BRAIN G[A

MW00784401

WHEEL of FORTUNE®

WORD PUZZLES

Publications International, Ltd.

ISBN: 978-1-63938-021-3

Manufactured in U.S.A.

8 7 6 5 4 3 2 1

Let's get social!
 @Publications_International
@PublicationsInternational
@BrainGames.TM
www.pilbooks.com

Puzzles from America's Game

Are you ready to uncover rhymes, occupations, places on the map, characters, and sayings? Put your Wheel of Fortune® wits to the test with *Brain Games® Wheel of Fortune® Word Puzzles*. These puzzles are perfect for anyone who has ever wanted to be a contestant on the popular American game show. Like the show, there are multiple subject categories to solve, and each puzzle will tell you how many letters are remaining. Remember, a letter can be used more than once when you're filling in the spaces. To keep things interesting, we've mixed in some other word-based puzzles. There's a new challenge on every page!

Answers can be found at the back of the book.

CHARACTER

Solve the puzzle using 5 remaining letters. HINT: Here comes Christopher Robin.

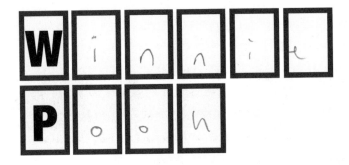

Answers on page 359.

PEOPLE

Solve the puzzle using 3 remaining letters. HINT: The beginning phase of a relationship.

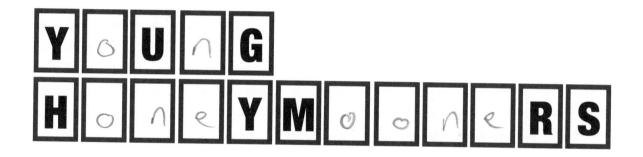

YOUNG
HONEYMOONERS

LIVING THINGS

Solve the puzzle using 6 remaining letters. HINT: One can have a huge ego about a mane.

A PRIDE OF LIONS

Answers on page 359.

LIVING THINGS

Solve the puzzle using 4 remaining letters. HINT: One hobby includes rummaging through the garbage.

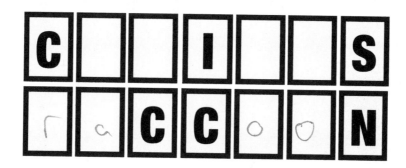

C			I			S
		C	C			N

CHARACTERS

Solve the puzzle using 3 remaining letters. HINT: There's no place like home.

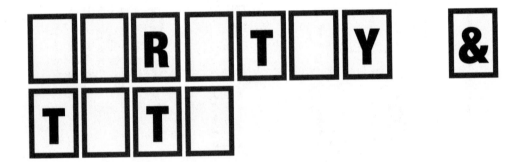

Answers on page 359.

AROUND THE HOUSE

Solve the puzzle using 4 remaining letters. HINT: Can cause physical harm if not carfeul.

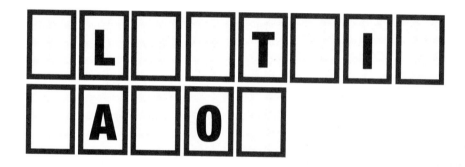

Answers on page 359.

FUN & GAMES

Solve the puzzle using 4 remaining letters. HINT: Hold on tight.

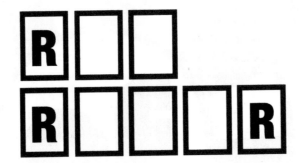

Answers on page 359.

CODE-DOKU

Solve this puzzle just as you would a sudoku. Use deductive logic to complete the grid so that each row, column, and 3 by 3 box contains the letters from the word GYMNASTIC.

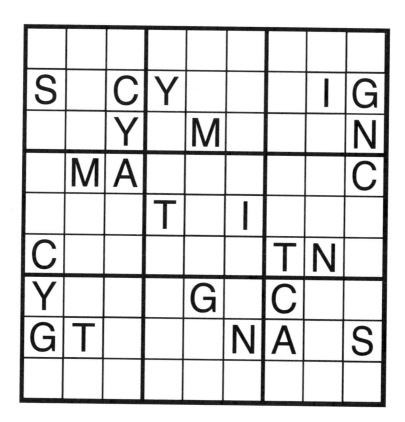

IN THE KITCHEN

Solve the puzzle using 5 remaining letters. HINT: It's important to have silverware with your meal.

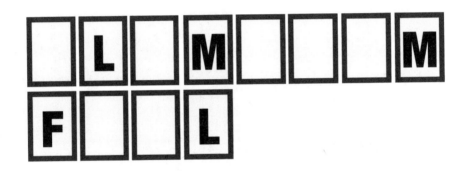

Answers on page 359.

FOOD & DRINK

Solve the puzzle using 3 remaining letters. HINT: Millennials enjoy this with a cup of coffee.

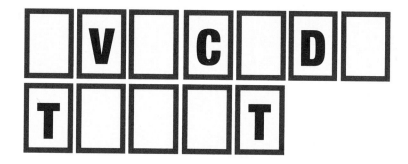

PROPER NAME

Solve the puzzle using 4 remaining letters. HINT: Pause.
It's time to meet the parents.

 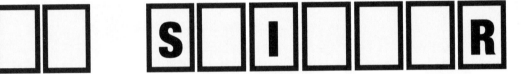

Answers on page 359.

LIVING THING

Solve the puzzle using 3 remaining letters. HINT: When a Red Sox's player fetches the baseball.

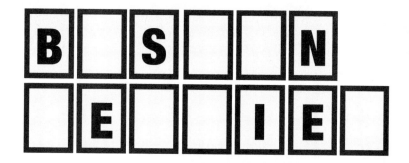

WHAT ARE YOU WEARING?

Solve the puzzle using 4 remaining letters. HINT:
Designed for lounging on your couch.

Answers on page 359.

PROPER NAMES

Solve the puzzle using 6 remaining letters. HINT: His Oscar-nominated 2014 work was out of this world.

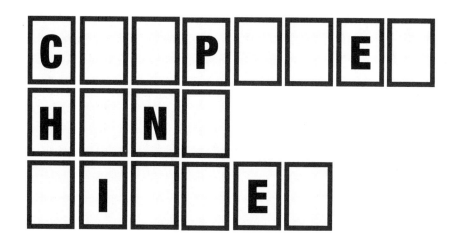

PHRASE

Solve the puzzle using 7 remaining letters. HINT: It's royally good.

Answers on page 359.

RHYME TIME

Solve the puzzle using 2 remaining letters. HINT: Wave
your wand.

SHOW BIZ

Solve the puzzle using 6 remaining letters. HINT: Lin-Manuel Miranda has been nominated for two Tonys.

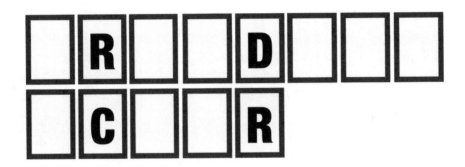

Answers on page 359.

OCCUPATION

Solve the puzzle using 4 remaining letters. HINT: Also known as a polite architect.

ADD-A-WORD

Add one word to each of the 3-word sets to create new words or phrases. For example: In a set including "smith," "fore," and "game," the added word would be "word" (creating "wordsmith," "foreword," and "word game").

1. question, time, skid: _____

2. collector, spoon, fold: _____

3. apple, amber, rabbit: _____

4. ground, wagon, wood: _____

5. pop, folk, gallery: _____

6. free, power, ill: _____

Answers on page 359.

PROPER NAMES

Solve the puzzle using 6 remaining letters. HINT: His popular science podcast was adapted into a TV show.

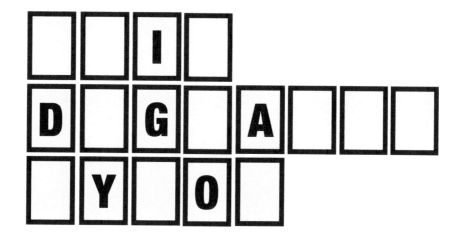

OFFICIAL INK

Travel in sequence through the puzzle from the left side to the right, using each numbered clue to determine the correct word. Connect adjacent words together with a common letter to proceed through the maze. Some letters are already given. The first and last words tie into the title.

1. Material of tires

2. Revolving part

3. Repeats a story

4. Broth

5. Out of money

6. Spoiled

7. Not nieces

8. Not a light matter

9. "On the _____ where you live"

10. Passage through a mountain

11. Within the law

12. Give money temporarily

13. Sink component

14. Draft (Brit.)

15. Tarnish

16. Hair

17. Postage

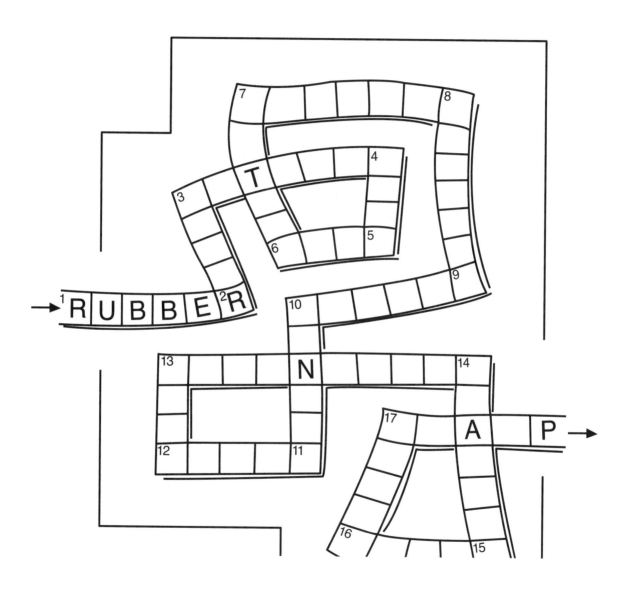

CROSSWORD

ACROSS

1. Check the bar code
5. Family chart
9. Blog entries
14. Teeny bit
15. Jazz great Hines
16. Mr. T's TV outfit
17. Deanna of "Star Trek: TNG"
18. Landers and Meara
19. Conk out, as a car
20. It has its ups and downs (No. 1)
23. Blown up, as a neg.
24. Arson evidence
25. FedEx arrival
28. These can be checkered
30. Jump causer
32. Backyard storage facility
33. Craven who directed "Swamp Thing"
35. "___ be in England": Browning
37. Butterworth or Doubtfire
38. It has its ups and downs (No. 2)
41. Pie-mode link
43. Knit's partner
44. Cpl. or Sgt.
45. Mazar of "GoodFellas"
47. Co. now part of Verizon
48. Carousel figure
52. Big rig fuel
54. Dish of roasted roots
56. Caboose's place
57. It has its ups and downs (No. 3)
61. Squeezed (out), as wet towels
63. Juice, so to speak: Abbr.
64. Bear whose porridge was too hot
65. Midler or Davis
66. Activist Parks
67. Novello of old films
68. Pacific salmon varieties
69. One in arrears
70. Put in the mail

DOWN

1. Military status account, briefly
2. Popular Mexican beer
3. Coral rings
4. Clip-and-file item
5. Salty drops
6. Cowboy's dressing?
7. Cube inventor Rubik
8. "Born Free" lioness
9. Linguini, for one
10. Frisky swimmers
11. "I haven't a clue"
12. Chess champion Mikhail
13. Opposite of lge.
21. Cut some slack
22. Exact, to a Brit
26. Always, in a poem
27. Joseph Smith's denom.
29 Snake-eyes number
30. "I Dreamed a Dream" singer Susan
31. Cry from one who just got the joke

34. Baby carrier brand
36. Boo-boo
38. Slugger of 714 homers
39. Old PC screen
40. "Barney Miller" actor Jack
41. Sum up
42. Island neckwear
46. Really enjoys
49. Make a backup copy, say
50. Easily attached accessory

51. R. Murrow or G. Robinson
53. Slight advantages
54. Bel ___ (Italian cheese)
55. Felix's "odd" friend
58. Fictional detective Wolfe
59. Gentle firelight, e.g.
60. Not Meth. or Presby.
61. Pugilist's org.
62. Bygone Olds

FUN & GAMES

Solve the puzzle using 6 remaining letters. HINT: Go directly to jail.

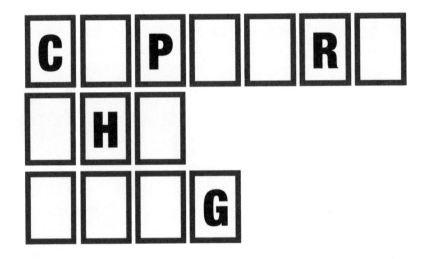

Answers on page 360.

ADD-A-WORD

Add one word to each of the 3-word sets to create new words or phrases. For example: In a set including "smith," "fore," and "game," the added word would be "word" (creating "wordsmith," "foreword," and "word game")

1. box, fox, gold: _____

2. air, battle, day: _____

3. pay, off, data: _____

4. ding, man, boy: _____

5. eye, gum, room: _____

6. dream, mate, work: _____

Answers on page 360.

FUN & GAMES

Solve the puzzle using 4 remaining letters. HINT: You must be this tall.

Answers on page 360.

FITTING WORDS

In this miniature crossword, the clues are listed randomly and are numbered for convenience only. It is up to you to figure out the placement of the 9 answers. To help you, we've inserted one letter in the grid, and this is the only occurrence of that letter in the completed puzzle.

1. Short skirt

2. Get nosy

3. "_____ the Rainbow"

4. Simplicity

5. Juliet's beloved

6. Good judgment

7. Change for a five

8. Birdlike

9. Coarse file

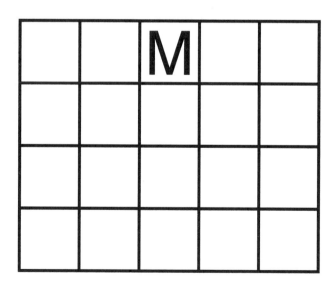

Answers on page 360.

EVENT

Solve the puzzle using 6 remaining letters. HINT:
Memorial Day, Independence Day, or Labor Day.

				R		
	O	I			Y	

Answers on page 360.

BEFORE & AFTER

Solve the puzzle using 7 remaining letters. HINT: There are no kings at college.

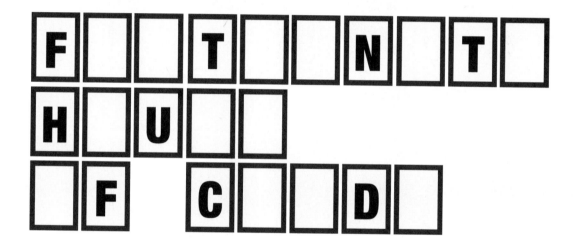

Answers on page 360.

Food & DRINK

Solve the puzzle using 4 remaining letters. HINT: Bare toast isn't meant to be preserved.

EVENT

Solve the puzzle using 6 remaining letters. HINT: A lyric duel.

PROPER NAMES

Solve the puzzle using 8 remaining letters. HINT: Her *Daily Show* appearances tend to go viral.

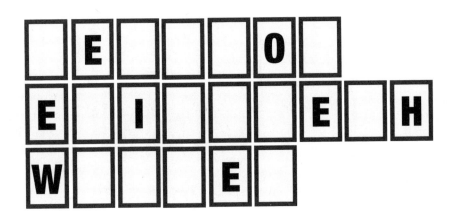

Answers on page 360.

ELEVATOR WORDS

Like an elevator, words move up and down the "floors" of this puzzle. Starting with the first answer, the second part of each answer carries down to become the first part of the following answer. With the clues given, complete the puzzle.

1. Great _____   1. Montana city

2. _____ _____   2. Retreats

3. _____ _____   3. Remote rural area

4. _____ _____   4. US is 1; UK is 44

5. _____ _____   5. Euphemism

6. _____ _____   6. Microsoft Word eclipsed it

7. _____ storm   7. Rare confluence

POINTS IN THE PAINT

Every word listed is found in the group of letters. Words can be in a straight line horizontally, vertically, or diagonally. They may be forward or backward.

ASSIST

BASKET

BLOCK

BUZZER

DOWNTOWN

DRAIN

DRIBBLE

DUNK

ELEVATION

FAKE

HALFTIME

HOOK

HOOP

JUMP

LANE

LOB

PASS

PERCENTAGE

PIVOT

REBOUND

RIM

ROLL

ROTATION

SHOT

STRATEGY

TECHNICAL

TEMPO

TRAVELING

TRIANGLE

ZONE

```
B  L  M  A  D  H  J  S  F  G  H  B  A  E  K  A  F
U  L  T  L  R  T  B  O  J  R  O  N  V  N  F  W  N
I  V  O  P  P  H  U  U  E  L  P  I  D  O  C  M  W
T  E  A  C  D  C  R  B  Z  O  M  V  D  Z  Y  K  O
O  K  W  G  K  J  O  E  O  Z  H  X  O  B  B  E  T
V  F  N  N  Q  U  L  H  U  L  E  U  J  P  R  L  N
I  E  O  U  N  O  L  Q  Y  Z  O  R  L  E  E  G  W
P  H  C  D  D  T  E  F  Y  W  O  V  A  R  C  N  O
Y  L  N  B  C  D  T  V  T  W  N  R  C  C  A  A  D
Y  R  J  J  A  S  E  R  R  O  X  N  I  E  E  I  F
G  G  C  P  D  Y  K  Z  I  E  D  N  N  N  L  R  M
N  L  F  G  X  G  S  T  K  O  O  H  H  T  E  T  F
I  P  Q  E  X  E  A  C  T  J  Z  S  C  A  V  K  V
L  A  M  C  F  T  B  P  E  S  C  A  E  G  A  O  Q
E  T  X  U  O  A  X  Z  H  F  I  N  T  E  T  W  U
V  L  E  R  J  R  O  Z  Q  R  G  S  G  B  I  B  S
A  H  B  M  C  T  X  D  R  A  I  N  S  G  O  H  S
R  T  R  B  P  S  V  Y  K  H  N  V  L  A  N  E  A
T  D  I  Z  P  O  I  S  H  O  T  K  M  R  T  B  P
N  E  M  H  A  L  F  T  I  M  E  L  B  B  I  R  D
```

Answers on page 361.

FUN & GAMES

Solve the puzzle using 9 remaining letters. HINT: These are very tiny areas of expertise.

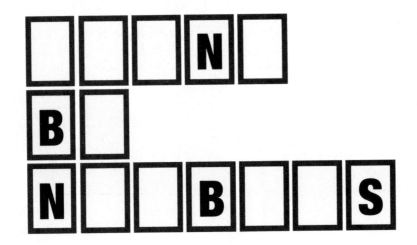

Answers on page 361.

THEME PARK

This "ride" has a theme, but we can't tell you what it is. Place all the words in the boxes below—when you do, read the word created in the outlined boxes, from top to bottom, to reveal what the theme is.

TREADMILL

DUMBBELLS

ROWER

BIKE

FREE WEIGHTS

ELLIPTICALS

CARDIO

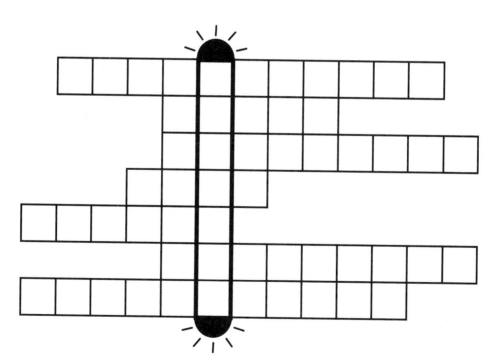

FOOD & DRINK

Solve the puzzle using 4 remaining letters. HINT: Before the shell on your ice cream becomes hard.

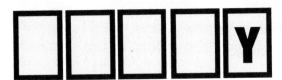 

Answers on page 361.

RHYME TIME

Solve the puzzle using 5 remaining letters. HINT: Salad toppings either loved or hated.

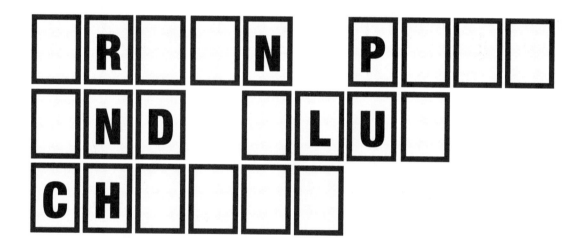

Answers on page 361.

REVOLVING ENTRANCE

Travel in sequence through the puzzle from the left side to the right, using each numbered clue to determine the correct word. Connect adjacent words together with a common letter to proceed through the maze. Some letters are already given. The first and last words tie into the title.

1. Change direction

2. Michael Jackson's "land"

3. Spoil

4. Special offering

5. Rainbow, speckled, or brown

6. Drink glass

7. Biggest

8. Lumber size

9. Meat glaze

10. Short hit

11. Chewy candy

12. Positive

13. Brother

14. Smile

15. Naked folks

16. Rescuer

17. Horse color

18. Small pests

19. Steps at a fence

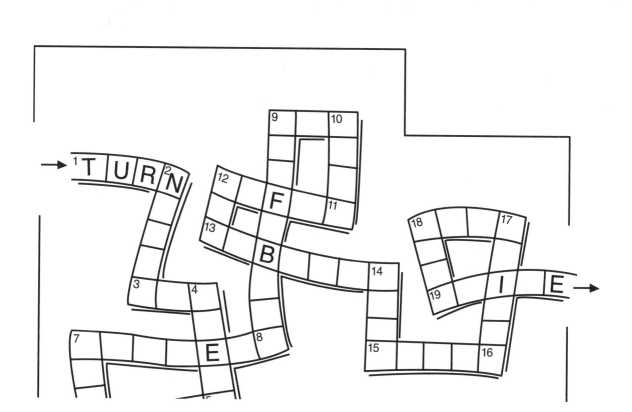

Answers on page 361.

AROUND THE HOUSE

Solve the puzzle using 5 remaining letters: HINT: All a risky dance needs is "Old Time Rock 'n Roll," socks, and somewhere to slide.

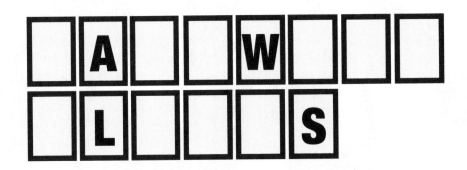

Answers on page 361.

SAME NAME

Solve the puzzle using 7 remaining letters. HINT: On a map there are infinite places one can go.

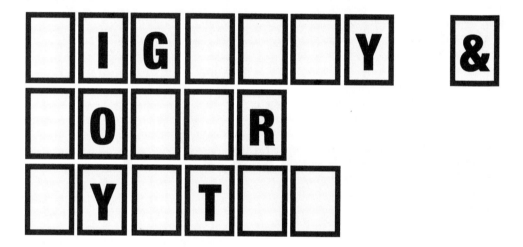

Answers on page 361.

OPPOSITES

Use the letters below to fill in the boxes and reveal the 2 related words. Connected boxes share the same letter.

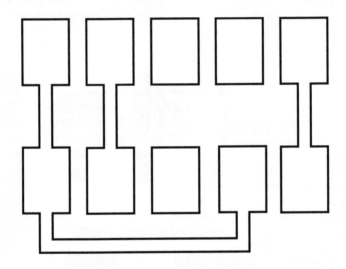

FLOTWY

Answers on page 361.

ADDAGRAM

These two puzzles function exactly like an anagram with an added step: In addition to being scrambled, each set of words below is missing the same letter. Discover the missing letter, then unscramble the words.

TACKER

MALKIN

SMILER

OCTANT

UNCOIL

RAZING

NUTRIA

FOOD & DRINK

Solve the puzzle using 5 remaining letters. HINT: Almost as good as having a cookie for breakfast.

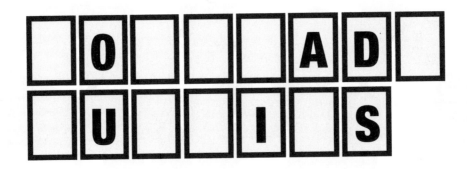

Answers on page 362.

PHRASE

Solve the puzzle using 4 remaining letters. HINT: Can't remember? Maybe these photos will help.

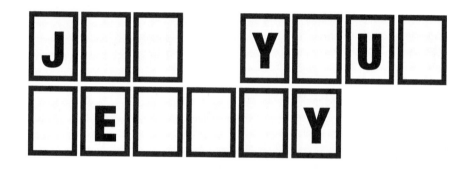

SAME LETTER

Solve the puzzle using 5 remaining letters. HINT: You may find it under the couch cushions.

Answers on page 362.

SPLIT DECISIONS

Fill in each set of empty cells with letters that will create English words reading both across and down. Letters may repeat within a single set. We've completed one set to get you started.

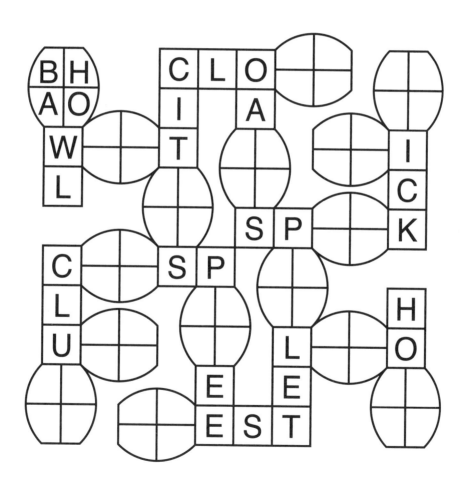

THINGS

Solve the puzzle using 6 remaining letters. HINT: The lines on a map.

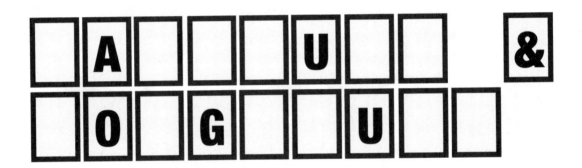

Answers on page 362.

ON THE MAP

Solve the puzzle using 5 remaining letters. HINT: Some badgers call it home.

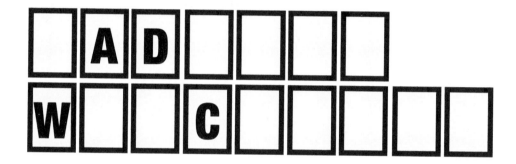

Answers on page 362.

LIVING THING

Solve the puzzle using 8 remaining letters. HINT: Has a life cycle of four stages.

Answers on page 362.

PROPER NAME

Solve the puzzle using 4 remaining letters. HINT: The old guitarist was feeling blue.

ADD-A-WORD

Add one word to each of the 3-word sets to create new words or phrases. For example: In a set including "smith," "fore," and "game," the added word would be "word" (creating "wordsmith," "foreword," and "word game").

1. quick, fish, screen: _____

2. flat, horse, pig: _____

3. rush, old, brick: _____

4. wool, band, pedal: _____

5. top, hat, ring: _____

6. plug, odeon, pumper: _____

Answers on page 362.

TITLE & AUTHOR

Solve the puzzle using 9 remaining letters. HINT: The movie adaptation of this sweeping modern take on *King Lear* was filmed in Rochelle, Illinois.

Row 1: ☐ ☐ ☐ ☐ U S ☐ ☐ D
Row 2: ☐ C R ☐ S ☐ B ☐ ☐
Row 3: J ☐ ☐ ☐ ☐ S ☐ I ☐ ☐ ☐

TITLE & AUTHOR

Solve the puzzle using 9 remaining letters. HINT: The movie adaptation of this sweeping modern take on *King Lear* was filmed in Rochelle, Illinois.

CROSSWORD

ACROSS

1. "Forever" post office product
6. Briny bodies
10. Duchamp's genre
14. Mr. Detoo
15. Just hanging, so to speak
16. Old musical high notes
17. Cartoon voicer Mel
18. Fill to capacity
19. "___ Island" (2008 Jodie Foster film)
20. "Beloved" author
23. Machu Picchu people
26. Leg shackles
27. Novel by 20-Across
32. Places for earrings
33. Bridge decline
34. Arrow trajectories
35. Hang loosely
36. Give a hoot
40. Offstage aides
41. Holmes of "Dawson's Creek"
42. Literature Nobelist, 1962
45. Hispaniola part
47. Fishing nets
48. Novel by 42-Across
53. Of the hipbone: Prefix
54. Like Rooster Cogburn's grit
55. Come to an end
59. Capitol VIPs
60. Give as a source
61. Dramatist Fugard
62. Diggs of "Private Practice"
63. Hinged fastener
64. One begins "The Lord is my shepherd"

DOWN

1. Day of rest: Abbr.
2. Oregon or Santa Fe: Abbr.
3. One-time connector
4. Artistic patchworks
5. Pennsylvania resort area
6. "Aye aye, capitán!"
7. Big cheese in Holland
8. A choir voice
9. One with powers of foresight
10. "The Godfather Part II" Oscar winner
11. "Foreign Affairs" novelist Lurie
12. Matt of "The Bourne Identity"
13. AARP and NCAA
21. Letters on a bounced check
22. Wheel accessories
23. "La ___ Bonita" (1987 Madonna hit)
24. Former Queen of Jordan
25. "The Suze Orman Show" channel
28. Fathers of foals
29. Dizzying drawings
30. Failure of judgment
31. Ending for many sugars
35. Bug for payment
36. Kitchen fixtures
37. "Got two fives for ___?"

38. Chinese side dish
39. Cartoon squeals
40. Fashionably smart
41. Patella
42. Disney cricket
43. Useless
44. Suffix of doctrines
45. Device for heavy lifting

46. Wouldn't hurt ___
49. Carve with acid
50. Diva's big number
51. Bar snacks
52. Far from shallow
56. "Caught in the act!"
57. Acapulco sun
58. Nightmare street of film

Answers on page 362.

SHAKESPEAREAN
CHARACTERS

Every name listed below is contained within the group of letters. Words can be found in a straight line horizontally, vertically, or diagonally. They may read either forward or backward.

AENEAS

ANTONY

BANQUO

CALPURNIA

CASSIO

CLEOPATRA

DEMETRIUS

FLAVIUS

GONERIL

HAMLET

HORATIO

HOTSPUR

IAGO

JULIET

LAERTES

MACBETH

MACDUFF

MERCUTIO

OPHELIA

OTHELLO

PERDITA

PERICLES

PORTIA

PRIAM

PROSPERO

PUCK

REGAN

ROMEO

SHYLOCK

ULYSSES

```
O R E P S O R P Q K J Z R G F
I S H H E G L Z K C O L Y H S
T E R M S A I N R U P L A C J
A T O M A I R P O P H E L I A
R R Z D E M E T R I U S X G H
O E E P N T N P A Y N O T N A
H A S G E H O T S P U R E F T
F L O I A R G I E T O T B F I
Y H L M T N B R T A J E E U D
F U L I E Y I A B U G S L D R
J E A W E C I Q N P C Y T C E
T R B O L U Z Y C Q S R B A P
G H T E B C A M Y S U X E M Z
C A S S I O L L E H T O X M R
Y F L A V I U S E L S F G C A
```

PERSON

Solve the puzzle using 5 remaining letters. HINT: Everything needs to be flawless.

`_ _ R F _ C _ O _ S _`

Answers on page 363.

WHAT ARE YOU DOING?

Solve the puzzle using 6 remaining letters. HINT: Set it to 375 degrees Fahrenheit before you put the cookies in.

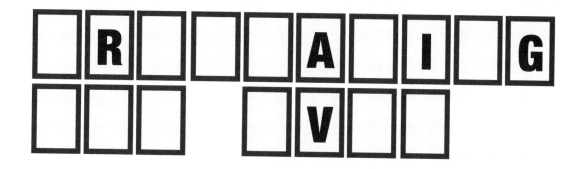

SAME LETTER

Solve the puzzle using 6 remaining letters. HINT: How tall is the Empire State Building?

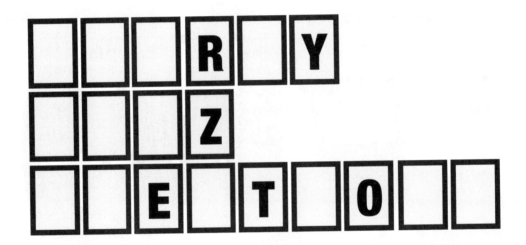

Answers on page 363.

PLACE

Solve the puzzle using 5 remaining letters. HINT: When vegetables grow above ground.

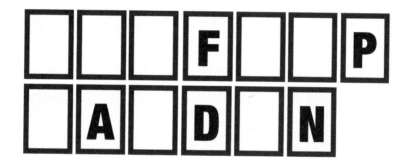

CODE-DOKU

Solve this puzzle just as you would a sudoku. Use deductive logic to complete the grid so that each row, column, and 3 by 3 box contains the letters AEJKLMOPS. When you have completed the puzzle, unscramble the letters to reveal the 11th president of the United States.

Answer:

L		E	M					J
	K				S			
O			L	P		M		E
		A				E		
P		S		M	K			O
		O		L		K		
		P		A	M		O	L
			E				M	
M			S					K

PROPER NAMES

Solve the puzzle using 5 remaining letters. HINT: His hit 2015 show won a Grammy Award.

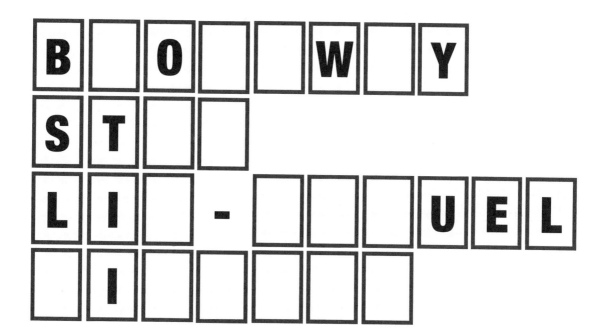

CROSSWORD

ACROSS
1. Nervous twitches
5. Macaroni, e.g.
10. Trudge through mud
14. At the peak of
15. Early Peruvian
16. "The forbidden fragrance," in ads
17. Nickname for Andrew Jackson
19. Barely gets by, with "out"
20. More crafty
21. Rife with foliage
22. A mosquito might leave one
23. Part of a stairway
25. Giraffe relatives
27. Urgent prompting
30. Handle, as a baton
31. Baboon cousins
32. Hyundai or Honda
35. Blunt, as reality
38. Boxing official, for short
39. "Hunches in Bunches" author
41. Actor's prompt
42. Yogurtlike Russian drink
44. Legal lead-in?
45. Barbed remark
46. Seed coats
48. Botanist Gregor
50. At an angle
52. Because of
54. Gobsmack
55. Pace at a track
57. Elicit a smile from
61. Big rig, for short
62. Beatles booster in the U.S.
64. High points for Heidi
65. Iridescent shell coating
66. Put in a mail slot
67. Pole on a sailing ship
68. Plane with no pilot
69. Macbeth trio

DOWN
1. Art colony near Santa Fe
2. "___ be all right"
3. Buffalo Bill
4. Crystal balls, for example
5. Photo, briefly
6. It's over a foot
7. Clean with steel wool
8. Does road work
9. "Be that as it may..."
10. Rod or Martha
11. Site of hockey's "miracle on ice"
12. Printer's daggers
13. Strong winds
18. 1998 Goo Goo Dolls hit
24. Dressing-room door ornament
26. Conical candy
27. Canine complaint
28. Fencer's foil
29. Imaginary pachyderms in "Winnie the Pooh"
30. Band's trip
33. "Snail mail" org.

34. Afternoon social
36. Goldberg of wacky contraptions
37. Nautical bottom
39. Case for a plumber
40. Daily order, with "the"
43. O. Henry, notably
45. Like trolls and some little mascots
47. Folk tale
49. "And others," briefly

50. Indian tea or state
51. Inscribed pillar
52. "Saturday Night Fever" joint
53. Driver's one-eighty
56. Hebrew month before Nisan
58. Colored eye part
59. Competed in "American Idol"
60. Odd's partners
63. Harper or Spike

Answers on page 363.

3-D WORD SEARCH

This puzzle follows the rules of your typical word search: Every last name (the first name for each being David) listed is contained within the group of letters. Words can be found in a straight line horizontally, vertically, or diagonally. They may read either forward or backward. But, in this version, words wrap up, down, and around the 3 sides of the cube.

BECKHAM

BIRNEY

BOWIE

BRENNER

BRINKLEY

BYRNE

CARRADINE

CASSIDY

CROSBY

DINKINS

DOYLE

FROST

GILMOUR

HALBERSTAM

HOCKNEY

LEISURE

LETTERMAN

LLOYD GEORGE

MAMET

MERRICK

NIVEN

RABE

SOUL

SOUTER

SPADE

STEINBERG

Answers on page 359.

TITLE & AUTHOR

Solve the puzzle using 6 remaining letters. HINT: Fictional detective Kinsey Millhone is once name-dropped by Melissa McCarthy's character on *Gilmore Girls*.

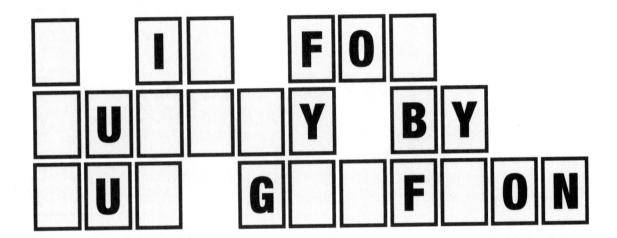

Answers on page 363.

ACROSTIC

Solve the clues below, and then place the letters in their corresponding spots in the grid to reveal a quote from Lisa Alther. The letter in the upper-right corner of each grid square refers to the clue the letter comes from. A black square indicates the end of a word.

A. Excessively energetic
62 3 15 56 52 43 48 51 46 33 63

B. On all _____
18 5 12 57 65

C. Offspring
47 7 60 54 14 35 24 50

D. Light-weight baseball alternative
59 39 30 45 55 32 27 1 37 13

E. Black _____ cake

44 29 40 8 58 6

F. Baton twirler
4 64 25 53 9 34 61 41 66

G. Graduated with _____
23 26 2 49 17 31

H. Shakespearean loverboy
42 11 21 16 19

I. Diamond measures
10 36 20 38 22 28

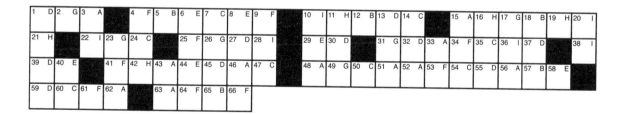

Answers on page 364.

SHROUDED SUMMARY

Hidden in the word search is a summary of a well-known novel. The words you need to find are listed below in alphabetical order; in the word search they are presented in an order that makes more sense. Words can be found in straight line horizontally, vertically, or diagonally. As a bonus, can you name the novel and its author?

AND	GUARD	SOLDIER
BECOME	IN	SPY
CARDINAL	INTRIGUE	THEY
CROSS	MALICIOUS	THREE
EMBROILED	NEWLY	WHEN
ENROLLED	PATHS	WITH
FEMALE	POLITICAL	WORKING
FOR	ROYAL	
FRIENDS	RUTHLESS	

Book title and author:

Y I R T U A R D E I L N W R A
R L I D S I F G M E A L T M U
N L W U R S K H B C N W L A K
P O O E N R O L L E D R A L D
W T R W N O H L R U T H K P E
H T K D J Y U M D P H C N C S
K N J G U A R D O I R P C L W
K O T H E L A E E S E F T D K
G U A R O N H L W N E R H Y H
S N L B L R U I N J M I B L L
L A C I T I L O P G E E Q O P
W H E N A Y O R N E C N R A S
J W C T H E Y B H O C D E P T
M L O R D S C M M E N S K F J
D E R I O R S E W S D P Y E S
N T A G T S U O I C I L A M H
U T I U E O S H T A P W N A N
W U Z E I L H R H P O E E L R
E Q W O S D O R E N Y P S E O
N F F J S C K G L W H U F B E
K M I L J A A F O R A V O E B
M I H T L I P R U T H L E S S
T L C D V T K F D G R Y P E T
E G O T E I Y W J I L D V G M
I A D S N R A P O A N U W O M
M L I G M D D L F K W A M C R
C I Y T R I T R L Y B V L Y T

77

FUN & GAMES

Solve the puzzle using 8 remaining letters. HINT: A lucrative career path when you're in elementary school.

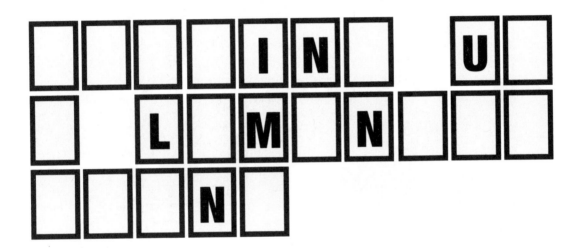

Answers on page 364.

WHAT ARE YOU DOING?

Solve the puzzle using 6 remaining letters. HINT: Sheryl Crow is going to tell everyone.

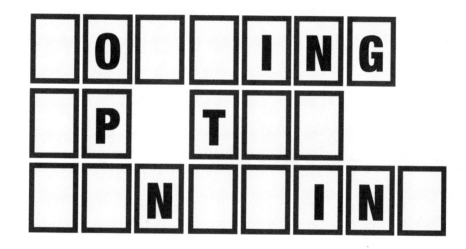

Answers on page 364.

FUN & GAMES

Solve the puzzle using 4 remaining letters. HINT: SpongeBob built a stand to teach this technique.

Answers on page 364.

THING

Solve the puzzle using 5 remaining letters. HINT: When a couple doesn't want an unexpected gift for their wedding.

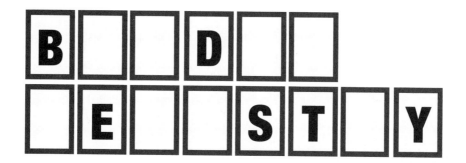

TITLE & AUTHOR

Solve the puzzle using 6 remaining letters. HINT: Pedants love to correct you about who this title character "really" is.

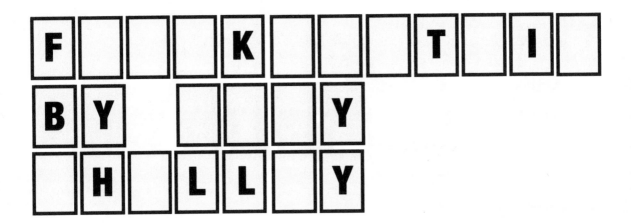

F				K				T		I	
B	Y					Y	
	H		L	L		Y

Answers on page 364.

ADD-A-WORD

Add one word to each of the 3-word sets to create new words or phrases. For example: In a set including "smith," "fore," and "game," the added word would be "word" (creating "wordsmith," "foreword," and "word game").

1. club, worm, cook: _____

2. sob, love, line:_____

3. folk, teller, tall:_____

4. boy, fair, down:_____

5. chain, love, opener:_____

6. pad, whole, foot:_____

Answers on page 364.

LIVING THINGS

Solve the puzzle using 7 remaining letters. HINT: Miss Baker was the first U.S. animal to fly into space and return safely.

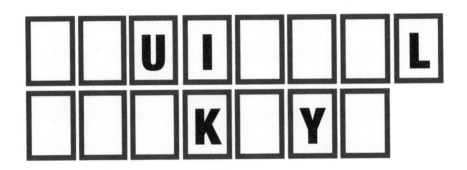

Answers on page 364.

RHYME TIME

Solve the puzzle using 3 remaining letters. HINT: Learning with a companion.

Answers on page 364.

PROPER NAMES

Solve the puzzle using 6 remaining letters. HINT: Still regal, though no longer regnant.

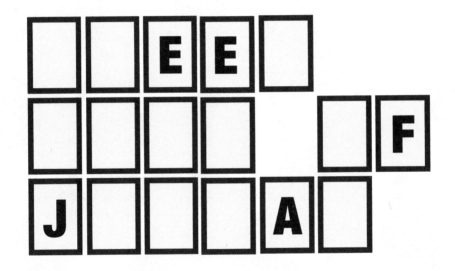

Answers on page 364.

FACES OF CHANGE

Fill in the blank spaces as you would a crossword puzzle. The theme—or title—of the puzzle might appear to be ambiguous, but it should suggest a category of words that, when linked together, will complete the puzzle.

For example, HOLE IN ONE might suggest DOUGHNUTS. Or, it might suggest GOLF, which would lead to the words CLUB, IRON, TEE, etc. But all of these words have a common theme. Notice that a few letters are already in place, and some of the words intersect—adding to the mystery, and the fun, of finding the solution.

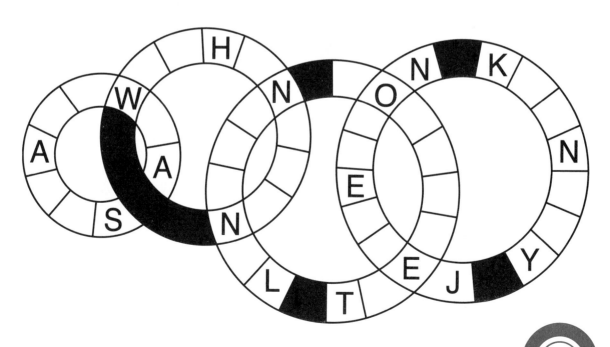

Answers on page 364.

BEFORE & AFTER

Solve the puzzle using 5 remaining letters. HINT: Fish definitely aren't found in a bathtub.

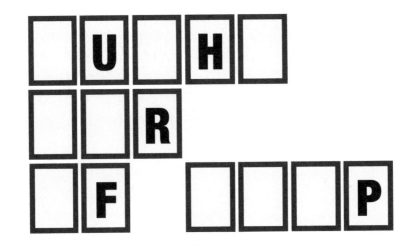

Answers on page 365.

CHARACTERS

Solve the puzzle using 6 remaining letters. HINT: Earth's mightest heroes.

FUN & GAMES

Solve the puzzle using 8 remaining letters. HINT: Stargaze from the comfort of your home.

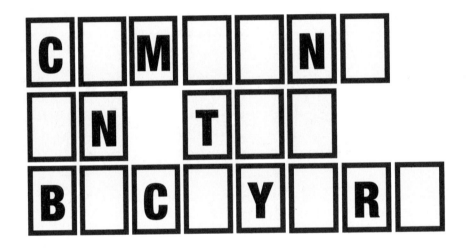

Answers on page 365.

FUN & GAMES

Solve the puzzle using 6 remaining letters. HINT: Grab them before the ocean tide rolls in.

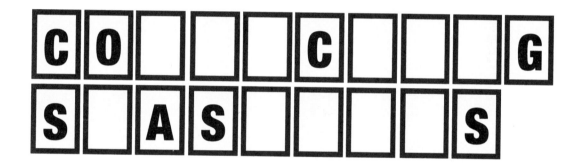

Answers on page 365.

PROPER NAMES

Solve the puzzle using 9 remaining letters. HINT:
Sometimes you feel like a nut.

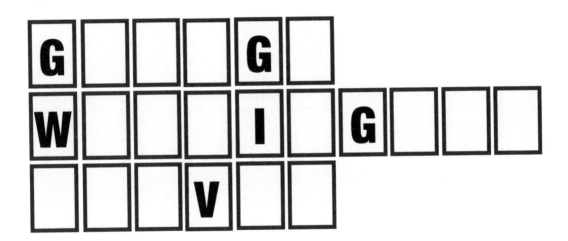

Answers on page 365.

FOOD & DRINK

Solve the puzzle using 7 remaining letters. HINT: Don't order this north of the Mason–Dixon.

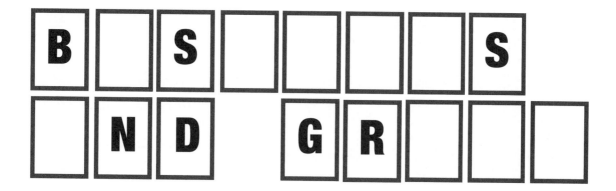

B | | S | | | | | S
| N | D | | G | R | | |

Answers on page 365.

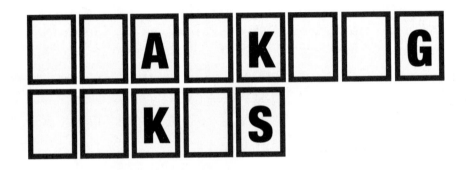

FUN & GAMES

Solve the puzzle using 7 remaining letters. HINT: Why did the chicken cross the road?

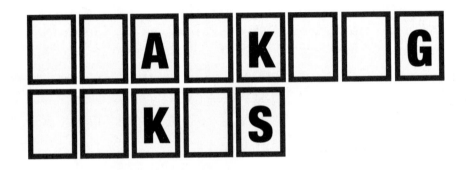

Answers on page 365.

FUN & GAMES

Solve the puzzle using 5 remaining letters. HINT: It takes two to...

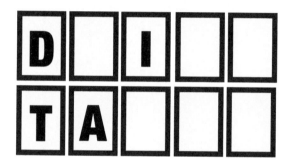

Answers on page 365.

PLACE

Solve the puzzle using 6 remaining letters. HINT: In the city, buy until the credit card hits decline.

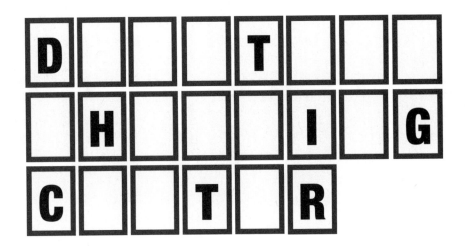

Answers on page 365.

LANDMARKS

Solve the puzzle using 5 remaining letters. HINT: Prominent Mexican archeological sites.

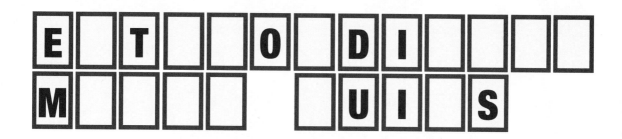

VEGETABLE TOGS

Fill in the blank spaces as you would a crossword puzzle. The theme or title of the puzzle might appear to be ambiguous, but it should suggest a category of words that, when linked together, will complete the puzzle. For example, HOLE IN ONE might suggest DOUGHNUTS. Or it might suggest GOLF, which would lead to the words CLUB, IRON, TEE, etc. But all of these words have a common theme. Notice that a few letters are already in place, and some of the words intersect, adding to the mystery and fun of finding the solution.

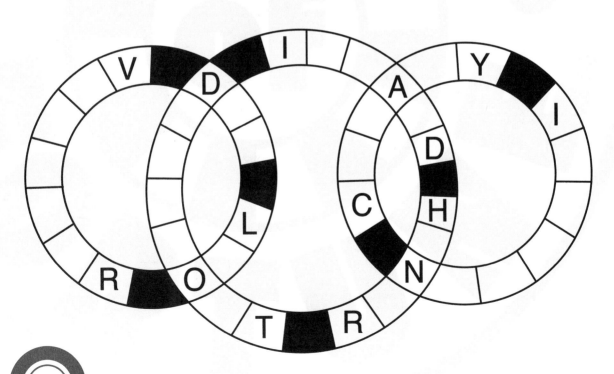

Answers on page 365.

LETTERBOX U.S. PRESIDENT

The letters in POLK can be found in boxes 7, 8, 13, and 23, but not necessarily in that order. The same is true for the other presidents' names listed below. Using the names and the box numbers that follow them to guide you, insert all the letters of the alphabet into the boxes. If you do this correctly, the shaded cells will reveal 2 more U.S. presidents.

Unused letter: Z

BUCHANAN: 2, 5, 10, 19, 20, 22
CARTER: 4, 5, 9, 10, 25
CLEVELAND: 1, 2, 5, 7, 10, 18, 25
FILLMORE: 7, 8, 9, 11, 12, 14, 25
JEFFERSON: 2, 3, 8, 9, 11, 21, 25
McKINLEY: 2, 6, 7, 10, 12, 14, 23, 25
NIXON: 2, 8, 12, 24
POLK: 7, 8, 13, 23
QUINCY ADAMS: 2, 5, 6, 10, 12, 14, 16, 18, 20, 21
REAGAN: 2, 5, 9, 17, 25
WASHINGTON: 2, 4, 5, 8, 12, 15, 17, 21, 22

1	2	3	4	5	6	7	8	9	10	11	12	13

14	15	16	17	18	19	20	21	22	23	24	25	26
												Z

LANDMARK

Solve the puzzle using 7 remaining letters. HINT: Contains Jefferson's draft of the Declaration of Independence.

Answers on page 365.

EVENT

Solve the puzzle using 6 remaining letters. HINT: The feeling of dropping on a rollar coaster.

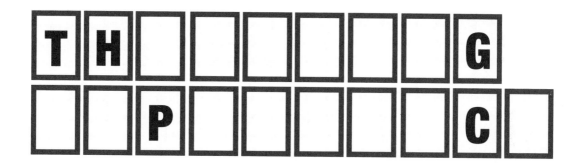

ELEVATOR WORDS

Like an elevator, words move up and down the "floors" of this puzzle. Starting with the first answer, the second part of each answer carries down to become the first part of the following answer. With the clues given, complete the puzzle.

1. Almond _____   1. Marzipan cousin

2. _____ _____   2. It's made to look like the real thing

3. _____ _____   3. Place for diamonds

4. _____ _____   4. Like some sales

5. _____ _____   5. Like some TVs

6. _____ _____   6. Something many an actress has

7. _____ dropper   7. One who pretends to know celebs

Answers on page 365.

FOOD & DRINK

Solve the puzzle using 4 remaining letters. HINT: For those who Lent a hand.

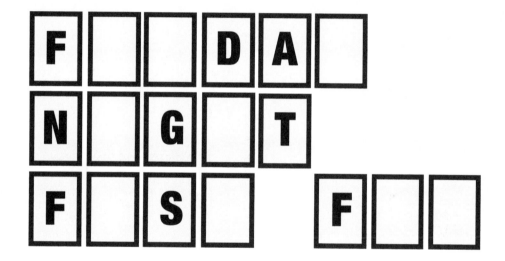

Answers on page 365.

CROSSWORD

ACROSS
1. "Hey, over here!"
5. Band blasters
9. Swanky events
14. Like a red tomato
15. Wad of cash
16. Love a lot
17. It's near Yemen
18. Small sewing case
19. Parkinson's med
20. Food they love in China
23. Grab some grub
24. Butter serving
25. Annie or Oliver Twist, e.g.
28. Become untangled
30. Ritual woodpile
32. Lennon's beloved
33. Audible range
36. Love handles, to put it nicely
37. Food they love in France
39. Appear
41. Gem or playing marble
42. Rainbow shape
43. "Comin' ___ the Rye" (Burns poem)
44. Freeway entrances
48. She loved Cupid
50. Bit of downhill gear
52. Deadeye's skill
53. Food they love in Mexico

57. Sadness, poetically
59. Pinta sister ship
60. Drudgery
61. Once-___ (quick appraisals)
62. Ear-related
63. Hammer or saw
64. West Point student
65. Vampire's target
66. Raggedy ___ (dolls)

DOWN
1. Investigates
2. Like apes or chimpanzees
3. Ancient rival of Athens
4. Look after
5. Game or circus setting
6. Church choir song
7. Positive end, battery-wise
8. Open, as a letter
9. In plentiful amounts
10. Make sense
11. Legal escape hatch
12. Jean ___, daddy of dada
13. Sailor's realm
21. Cousin of kerplunk
22. Combat mission
26. Santa ___ (Western wind)
27. Fat cat, in British slang
29. Paper purchase
30. Flickr image
31. Thank-___ (gift acknowledgements)
34. Friend of Monica and Phoebe
35. Overhead light
36. Jumpy bug

37. Used, and used again
38. Tune's text
39. Sitting duck
40. Sounds of hesitation
43. Desire for water
45. Leave stranded
46. Rack and ___ steering
47. Seems suspicious

49. Routine task
50. Kind of boom
51. Flair
54. Privy to
55. Issue a ticket to
56. "___ girl!" ("Way to go!")
57. Bashful buddy?
58. Eggs, to Ovid

1	2	3	4		5	6	7	8		9	10	11	12	13
14					15					16				
17					18					19				
20				21				22						
23				24				25				26	27
28			29			30	31				32		
		33		34	35					36			
	37								38				
39	40			41									
42			43					44		45	46	47
48			49				50	51			52		
	53				54	55				56			
57	58				59					60			
61					62					63			
64					65					66			

Answers on page 365.

BEFORE & AFTER

Solve the puzzle using 7 remaining letters. HINT: The Maverick waves.

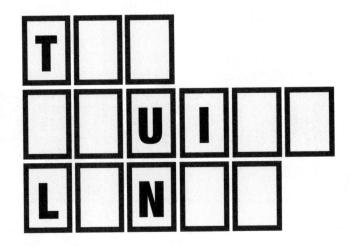

ON THE MAP

Solve the puzzle using 4 remaining letters. HINT: Billy Joel once said this city will wait for you.

FOOD & DRINK

Solve the puzzle using 4 remaining letters. HINT: Add a sliver of excitement to your meal.

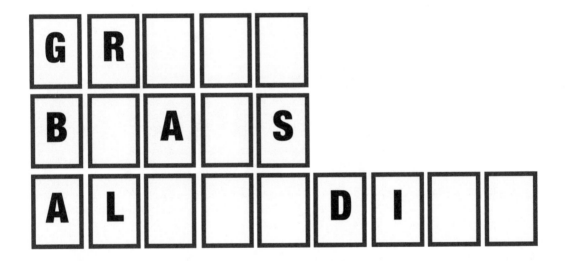

Answers on page 366.

ADD-A-WORD

Add one word to each of the 3-word sets to create new words or phrases. For example: In a set including "smith," "fore," and "game," the added word would be "word" (creating "wordsmith," "foreword," and "word game").

1. couch, chip, sweet: _____

2. mill, bell, mint: _____

3. seat, second, split: _____

4. pole, green, bag: _____

5. dome, skin, yellow: _____

6. paper, paddy, wild: _____

109

PERSON

Solve the puzzle using 5 remaining letters. HINT: There is a musician on the roof.

Answers on page 366.

OCCUPATION

Solve the puzzle using 5 remaining letters. HINT: Expensive sofas and chairs.

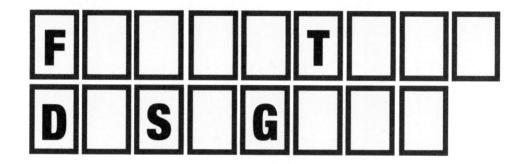

WHAT ARE YOU DOING?

Solve the puzzle using 7 remaining letters. HINT: If you eat the whole bread basket, you won't finish your meal.

Answers on page 366.

RHYME TIME

Solve the puzzle using 4 remaining letters. Hint: Vastly different in size.

OPPOSITES

Use the letters below to fill in the boxes and reveal the 2 related words. Connected boxes share the same letter.

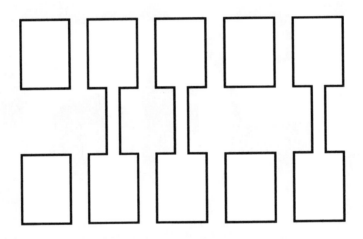

ADELRTY

Answers on page 366.

BEFORE & AFTER

Solve the puzzle using 6 remaining letters. HINT: Usually made of ground "Chuck"?

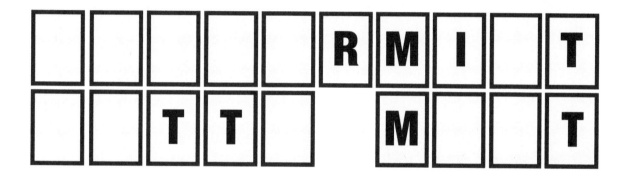

EVENT

Solve the puzzle using 6 remaining letters. HINT: Make sure to throw your cap toward the sky.

Answers on page 366.

PHRASE

Solve the puzzle using 5 remaining letters. HINT: In December we say, 5...4...3...2...1...

ELEVATOR WORDS

Like an elevator, words move up and down the "floors" of this puzzle. Starting with the first answer, the second part of each answer carries down to become the first part of the following answer. With the clues given, complete the puzzle.

1. Minute _____

2. _____ _____

3. _____ _____

4. _____ _____

5. _____ _____

6. _____ _____

7. _____ bearing

1. Part of a corporation's records

2. Readers' group

3. It may be cooked medium

4. Place to get last entry

5. Oil- or water-based purchase

6. It may be used to apply previous entry

7. Machine part

118

Answers on page 366.

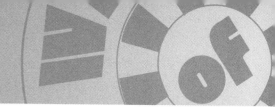

LIVING THING

Solve the puzzle using 6 remaining letters. HINT: Sebastian's distant relative.

FITTING WORDS

In this miniature crossword, the clues are listed randomly and are numbered for convenience only. It is up to you to figure out the placement of the 9 answers. To help you, we've inserted one letter in the grid, and this is the only occurrence of that letter in the completed puzzle.

1. Heavenly glow
2. Sound transmission
3. Pinball no-no
4. Figure of Scandinavian folklore
5. Singer _____ Domino
6. Devout
7. Religion
8. Fan favorite
9. Like potato chips or pretzels

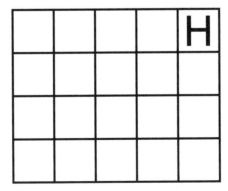

Answers on page 366.

FOOD & DRINK

Solve the puzzle using 7 remaining letters. HINT: In a pinch, they count as a health food.

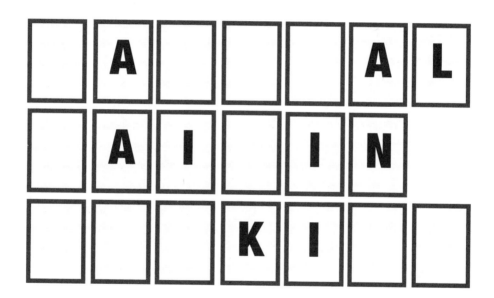

THINGS

Solve the puzzle using 4 remaining letters. HINT: Grab a duster and uncover.

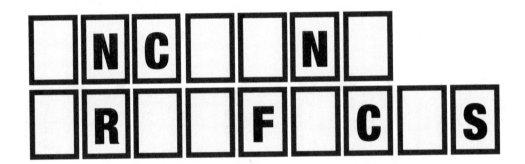

Answers on page 366.

LIVING THINGS

Solve the puzzle using 4 remaining letters. HINT: Spot these to avoid six more weeks of winter.

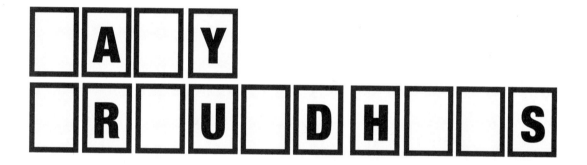

CROSSWORD

ACROSS

1. Unlike a gut course
5. Stared, as in wonder
10. Chanel, to friends
14. Lake that sounds creepy?
15. Colorful Greek salad bit
16. Calla lily
17. Colorful seafood entree
19. Mumbai wrap
20. Moisten, as a turkey
21. Zeus's jealous wife
22. Petulant state
23. Sitar pieces
25. They may be mental
27. Sweater wool
30. ___ and well (still kicking)
31. The V in VIP
32. "Once ___ a midnight ..."
35. Spanish bar snacks
38. Ram's ma'am
39. Colorful dessert treat
41. Psychic's claim
42. Dictation taker
44. Bacon chunk
45. Dole (out)
46. Group of nine
48. Leaning to the right
50. Neatnik's opposite
52. Tired of it all
54. Cabin wood

55. Quite a way off
57. Jewel box enclosure
61. Having reclined
62. Colorful salad topping
64. Ox seen in crosswords
65. Slow, in music
66. Relative of a wheeze
67. Cures rawhide
68. Downed, as a meal
69. Coin opening

DOWN

1. Parsley or sage
2. Square footage
3. Disposes (of)
4. Lay waste to
5. India's smallest state
6. Dominant wolf
7. Voice, slangily
8. "Thanks ___ so much"
9. Go off track
10. Tapioca plant
11. Colorful drink garnish
12. Madame of radium fame
13. Leaves out
18. Close by
24. Wild bovine of southeastern Asia
26. Tiny critter
27. NYC's Mad. and Lex.
28. Small salamander
29. Colorful salad ingredient
30. Kournikova of tennis
33. Hitching place

34. Hooter
36. Italian wine region
37. On ___ (without a contract)
39. Paleontologist's discovery
40. Footnote abbr.
43. Nine-day prayers
45. Red dyes
47. Empower
49. "Rambling Wreck From Georgia ___"

50. Water balloon sound
51. Jungle vine
52. Short trip
53. Rugged ridge
56. Pesky biter
58. Not fake
59. Capital on a fjord
60. Keep a tryst
63. Swindle

FOOD & DRINK

Solve the puzzle using 5 remaining letters. HINT: Our greatest innovations stem from "toss in olive oil to coat."

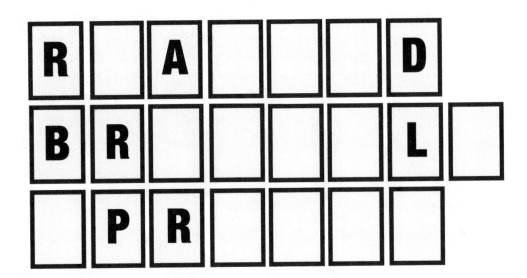

Answers on page 366.

LIVING THING

Solve the puzzle using 4 remaining letters. HINT: The hungry hungry...

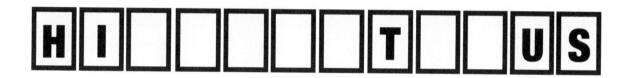

| H | I | | | | | | T | | | U | S |

Answers on page 367.

WORLD CITIES LETTERBOX

The letters in LONDON can be found in boxes 3, 10, 16, and 26, but not necessarily in that order. The same is true for the other cities listed below. Insert all the letters of the alphabet into the boxes. If you do this correctly, the shaded cells will reveal another world city.

Hint: Look for words that share a single letter. For example, ROME shares an O with SOFIA and an E with QUEBEC. By comparing the number lists following these 3 words, you can deduce the values of the 2 shared letters.

BRUSSELS: 7, 9, 18, 19, 21, 26

COPENHAGEN: 1, 3, 4, 5, 6, 16, 18, 24

HELSINKI: 1, 8, 9, 13, 16, 18, 26

JAKARTA: 2, 6, 7, 13, 20

LONDON: 3, 10, 16, 26

MEXICO CITY: 3, 4, 8, 15, 18, 20, 22, 23

QUEBEC: 4, 14, 18, 19, 21

QUEZON CITY: 3, 4, 8, 14, 15, 16, 17, 18, 19, 20

REYKJAVIK: 2, 6, 7, 8, 11, 13, 15, 18

ROME: 3, 7, 18, 23

SANTIAGO: 3, 6, 8, 9, 16, 20, 24

SOFIA: 3, 6, 8, 9, 12

VILNIUS: 8, 9, 11, 16, 19, 26

WARSAW: 6, 7, 9, 25

1	2	3	4	5	6	7	8	9	10	11	12	13

14	15	16	17	18	19	20	21	22	23	24	25	26

Answers on page 367.

ON THE MAP

Solve the puzzle using 4 remaining letters. HINT: There are actually more than 20 islands in total.

Answers on page 367.

ON THE MAP

Solve the puzzle using 6 remaining letters. HINT: Its flag features a triskelion, a symbol made of three rotating legs.

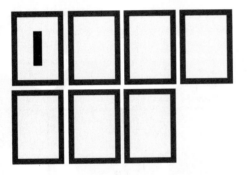

Answers on page 367.

CODE-DOKU

Solve this puzzle just as you would a sudoku puzzle. Use deductive logic to complete the grid so that each row, column, and 3 by 3 box contains the letters from the word TRAVELING.

	L						V	
			E	L				G
	V	I				E	T	
	N	G			R	T		
			A		I			
		V	L			N	A	
	G	N				A	I	
E			I	R				
	A						E	

131

Answers on page 367.

THINGS

Solve the puzzle using 6 remaining letters. HINT: Make sure to stay grounded when you turn a year older.

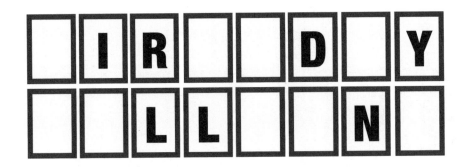

Answers on page 367.

SAME NAME

Solve the puzzle using 7 remaining letters. HINT: Many resturants have a special brunch on the weekends.

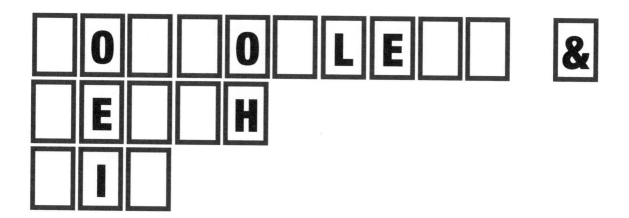

ACROSTIC

Solve the clues below, and then place the letters in their corresponding spots in the grid to reveal a quote by Thomas Carlyle. The letter in the upper-right corner of each grid square refers to the clue the letter comes from. A black square indicates the end of a word.

A. Shoulder covering
49 15 58 68 11

B. Not hindered or held back
7 51 67 25 60 40 1 37 54 70 18 72

C. Paperbundle
39 66 45 2 12

D. In a cryptic manner
21 31 19 27 29 46 48 16 33 56 71 5

E. Desert danger
8 13 43 20 62 42 59 17 24 3 47

F. Allegiance affirmations
50 22 65 28 9

G. Newlyweds, often
44 32 14 4 36 34 6 69 23 10 57 55

H. "Fight or Flight" chemical
61 26 41 38 30 35 53 63 64 52

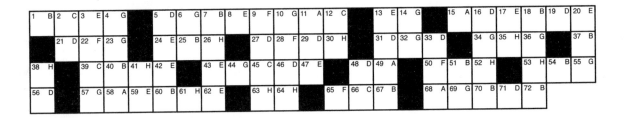

1 B	2 C	3 E	4 G		5 D	6 G	7 B	8 E	9 F	10 G	11 A	12 C		13 E	14 G		15 A	16 D	17 E	18 B	19 D	20 E
	21 D	22 F	23 G		24 E	25 B	26 H		27 D	28 F	29 D	30 H		31 D	32 G	33 D		34 G	35 H	36 G		37 B
38 H		39 C	40 B	41 H	42 E		43 E	44 G	45 C	46 D	47 E		48 D	49 A		50 F	51 B	52 H		53 H	54 B	55 G
56 D		57 G	58 A	59 E	60 B	61 H	62 E		63 H	64 H		65 F	66 C	67 B		68 A	69 G	70 B	71 D	72 B

TITLE & AUTHOR

Solve the puzzle using 5 remaining letters. HINT: After recording the audiobook herself, she was nominated for a Grammy Award.

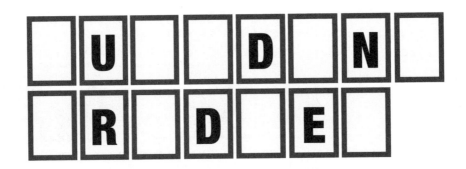

WHAT ARE YOU DOING?

Solve the puzzle using 5 remaining letters. HINT: The only similarity between San Francisco and Brooklyn other than high rent.

Answers on page 367.

PROPER NAME

Solve the puzzle using 6 remaining letters. HINT: Behind the iconic phrase "Well, Do Ya Punk?"

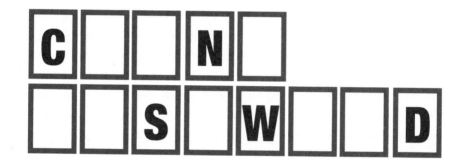

C _ _ N _
_ _ S _ W _ _ D

CODE-DOKU

Solve this puzzle just as you would a sudoku. Use deductive logic to complete the grid so that each row, column, and 3 by 3 box contains the letters from the word PUBLISHER.

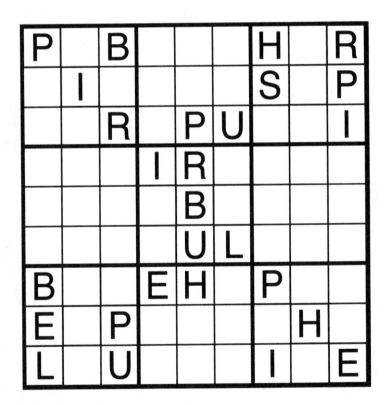

Answers on page 367.

ELEVATOR WORDS

Like an elevator, words move up and down the "floors" of this puzzle. Starting with the first answer, the second part of each answer carries down to become the first part of the following answer. With the clues given, complete the puzzle.

1. Broad _____

2. _____ _____

3. _____ _____

4. _____ _____

5. _____ _____

6. _____ _____

7. _____ slate

1. Daily publication

2. Pianist's reference

3. Teen's entertainment

4. Arcade item

5. Conclusion of a tennis contest

6. At close range

7. Tabula rasa

Answers on page 367.

139

DIAMOND CUT

Follow the arrows to solve each clue and complete the grid.

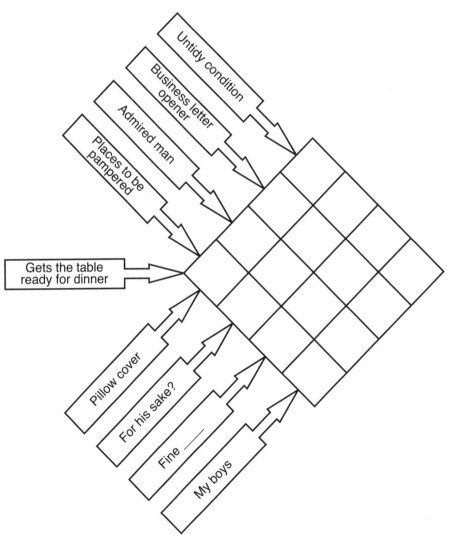

Answers on page 368.

SAME NAME

Solve the puzzle using 7 remaining letters. HINT: Penguins have elaborate ways to find each other after being separated for months.

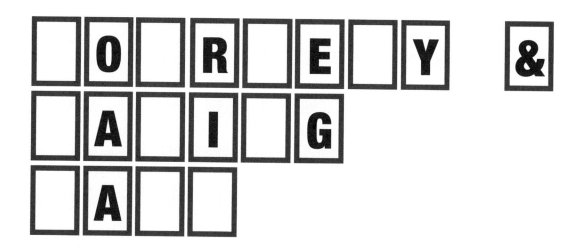

PROPER NAME

Solve the puzzle using 4 remaining letters. HINT: Touch down in Colorado.

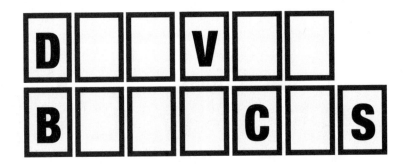

Answers on page 368.

AROUND THE HOUSE

Solve the puzzle using 5 remaining letters. HINT: A bed made for a queen.

THING

Solve the puzzle using 7 remaining letters. HINT: It was the best of times, it was the worst of times.

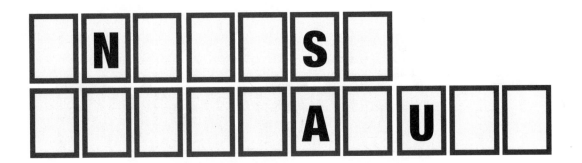

Answers on page 368.

CHARACTER

Solve the puzzle using 4 remaining letters. HINT: Leave it to Nancy Drew.

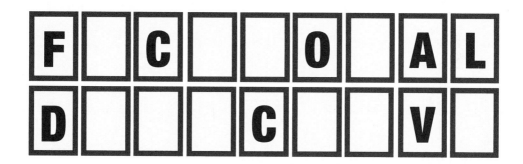

F _ C _ _ O _ A L
D _ _ _ C _ _ V _

FOOD & DRINK

Solve the puzzle using 5 remaining letters. HINT:
Neopolitan, but not ice cream.

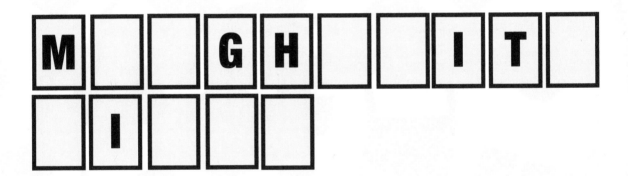

RHYME TIME

Each clue leads to a 2-word answer that rhymes, such as BIG PIG or STABLE TABLE. The numbers in parentheses after the clue give the number of letters in each word. For example, "cookware taken from the oven (3, 3)" would be "hot pot."

1. Smaller period in basketball or football (7, 7):

2. Dinner for an ocean-loving mammal (4, 4):

3. Outfit made from banana peels (5, 4):

4. Swamp mist (3, 3):

5. Strange facial hair (5, 5):

6. Jelly made from shelled seafood (4, 3):

7. Color of a female sheep (3, 3):

8. Room for storing pepper's counterpart (4, 5):

9. Smarter money-grubber (5, 5):

10. Intelligent beginning (5, 5):

11. Thin Timothy (4, 3):

12. Border wall with no hollow parts (5, 5):

13. Energetic celebration (6, 5):

14. Casper's bragging (6, 6):

15. The number one police officer (3, 3):

Answers on page 368.

ELEVATOR WORDS

Like an elevator, words move up and down the "floors" of this puzzle. Starting with the first answer, the second part of each answer carries down to become the first part of the following answer. With the clues given, complete the puzzle.

1. Pitch _____

2. _____ _____

3. _____ _____

4. _____ _____

5. _____ _____

6. _____ _____

7. _____ numeral

1. This may be used to get the band started

2. Don Quixote-like vision

3. They're simply the best

4. Collective desire to win

5. Adhesive used to attach false hair to skin

6. Substance obtained from acacia trees

7. One of several that appear with this puzzle

Answers on page 368.

BEFORE & AFTER

Solve the puzzle using 6 remaining letters. HINT: Crispy on the outside, Parisian on the inside.

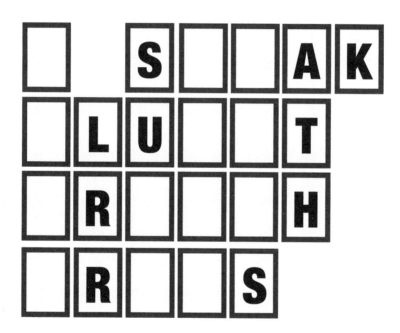

WHAT ARE YOU DOING?

Solve the puzzle using 5 remaining letters. HINT: Head to the nearest beach, sit back, and relax.

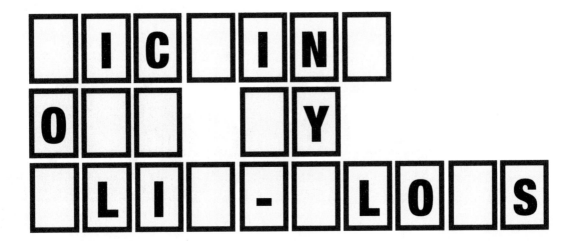

Row 1: ☐ I C ☐ I N ☐

Row 2: O ☐ ☐ ☐ Y

Row 3: ☐ L I ☐ - ☐ L O ☐ S

150

Answers on page 368.

OCCUPATION

Solve the puzzle using 6 remaining letters. HINT: It's important to listen to this person in case of a natural disaster.

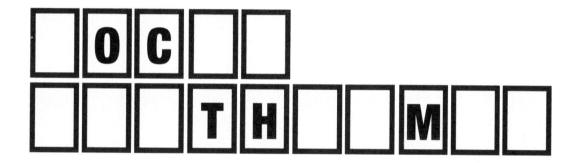

Answers on page 368.

FOOD & DRINK

Solve the puzzle using 6 remaining letters. HINT: Old cucumbers coated in oil.

Answers on page 368.

LIVING THING

Solve the puzzle using 4 remaining letters. HINT: Antelopes that live in Africa and Asia.

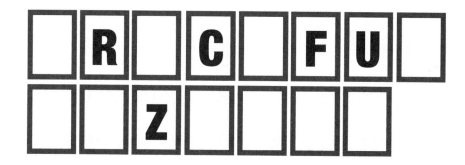

Answers on page 368.

RHYME TIME

Solve the puzzle using 5 remaining letters. HINT: It's definitely not a sunburn.

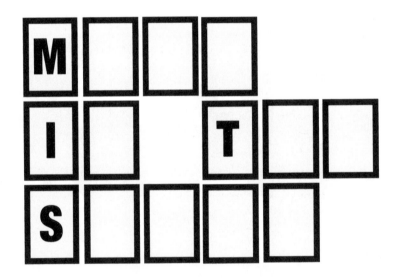

Answers on page 368.

RHYME TIME

Each clue leads to a 2-word answer that rhymes, such as BIG PIG or STABLE TABLE. The numbers in parentheses after the clue give the number of letters in each word.

1. Microsoft mogul Bill glides across the ice (5, 6):

gates Skates

2. Course of study taught by fashion designer Bill (5, 5):

Blast class

3. Cause "Groundhog Day" star Bill to fret (6, 5):

murray Worry

4. "Shake, Rattle and Roll" singer Bill's Sunday through Saturday newspapers (6, 7):

5. Former U.S. President Bill droppin' a clue (7, 6):

Hintin Clinton

Answers on page 368.

155

PEOPLE

Solve the puzzle using 7 remaining letters. HINT: Opening presents is likely to put a smile on their face.

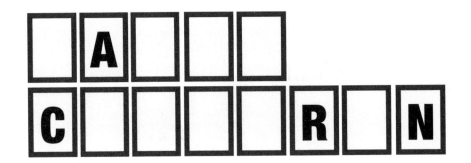

Answers on page 368.

CHARACTER

Solve the puzzle using 3 remaining letters. HINT: Magic strikes with lightning.

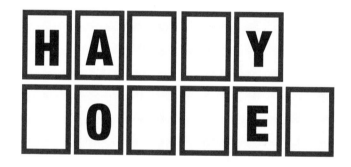

Answers on page 368.

WHAT ARE YOU WEARING?

Solve the puzzle using 5 remaining letters. HINT: Items necessary before you start the Appalachian Trail.

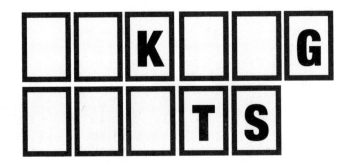

Answers on page 368.

PROPER NAME

Solve the puzzle using 5 remaining letters. HINT: Holds the Guinness World Record for longest career as a live-action Marvel super hero.

RHYME TIME

Each clue leads to a 2-word answer that rhymes, such as BIG PIG or STABLE TABLE. The numbers in parentheses after the clue give the number of letters in each word. We've done the first one for you.

1. Most superior bird's home (4, 4):
BEST NEST

2. Give sustenance to a warhorse (4, 5):

3. Forests owned by Robin of Sherwood Forest (5, 5):

4. Stage performer's farm vehicles (6, 8):

5. Actively against asking the big question (8, 9):

Answers on page 369.

RHYME TIME

Solve the puzzle using 6 remaining letters. HINT: The strategy of Melanie Griffith's *Working Girl*.

A POET & DIDN'T KNOW IT

Every word listed is contained within the group of letters. Words can be found in a straight line horizontally, vertically, or diagonally. They may be read either forward or backward.

ACROSTIC

ALLEGORY

ANAPEST

BALLAD

CADENCE

CANTO

DOGGEREL

ELEGY

ENJAMBMENT

EPIC

HAIKU

HEXAMETER

HYMN

IAMB

LIMERICK

LYRIC

MADRIGAL

METER

OCTAVE

ODE

ONOMATOPOEIA

PALINDROME

PANEGYRIC

PENTAMETER

RHYME

RONDEAU

SCANSION

SONNET

STANZA

VERSE

```
N P A L I N D R O M E C I U G Y N
M M P A N T H K O O X I H S E C U
Y D M Z K I N E S N H P U A I K X
H B X D E T J E X E D E P R I Z K
S C A N S I O N M A W E Y I A K Z
L A G I R D A M T B M L A V J A U
W F Y K E J B Z S V M E Y U Q F J
D B V V V A B R E U T A T E E C Z
O Y W O L J G E P S E A J E M G J
G S J L R L K T A C T K W N R L E
G P A H F B R E N A S A J X E D K
E D Y R E T E M A N O Q N N O C Z
R M L U O X W A C T N A I Z I Y C
E X E L E G Y T E O N V M R A R M
L C E C A D E N C E E N E K J O W
J D H C J Y E E H I T M N I C G N
O N O M A T O P O E I A U U B E I
P A N E G Y R I C L T L D H V L P
O C T A V E Q C P Z N E R Q E L R
B C M M W L L C I T S O R C A A R
```

FITTING WORDS

In this miniature crossword, the clues are listed randomly and are numbered for convenience only. It is up to you to figure out the placement of the 9 answers. To help you out, we've inserted one letter in the grid, and this is the only occurrence of that letter in the puzzle.

1. Youngsters

2. Elm or maple

3. In the know

4. Addlebrained

5. Gem surface

6. Pool table triangle

7. Pub game

8. Complete collections

9. On vacation

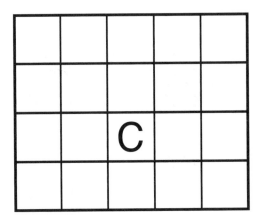

Answers on page 369.

CODE-DOKU

Solve this puzzle just as you would a sudoku. Use deductive logic to complete the grid so that each row, column, and 3 by 3 box contains the letters A D E I L O S T V. When you have completed the puzzle, unscramble the letters to reveal a word used to define interlocking joints used in woodworking.

Answer:

	D					A	
		S				L		V
O			S	D				T
			A	V	O			L
			L		I			
A				T				
L			O		A			D
D		T				E	
	S						O

Answers on page 369.

FOOD & DRINK

Solve the puzzle using 6 remaining letters. HINT: Either comes out burnt or half full.

M	C				A		E
			C			N	

Answers on page 369.

LANDMARK

Solve the puzzle using 4 remaining letters. HINT: Where Jim and Pam offically got married in *The Office*.

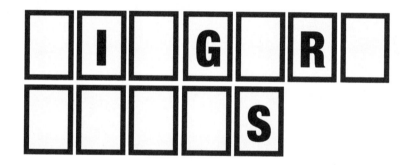

Answers on page 369.

LIVING THING

Solve the puzzle using 8 remaining letters. HINT: May have a tin ear . . . or a Rin Tin Tin ear.

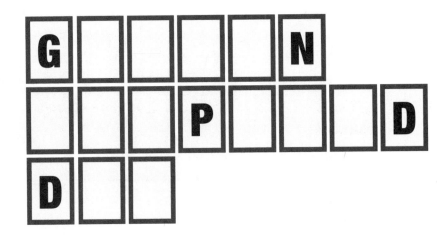

Answers on page 369.

FITTING WORDS

In this miniature crossword, the clues are listed randomly and are numbered only for convenience. Figure out the placement of the 9 answers. To help you out, 1 letter is inserted in the grid, and this is the only occurrence of that letter in the completed puzzle.

1. Sunburn soother

2. Great Barrier Reef material

3. Unaccompanied

4. Prepare for a trip

5. Slippery swimmers

6. Retains

7. Achy

8. Old hat

9. _____, crackle, pop

			S	
			N	
C	O	R	A	L
			P	

ANCIENT ANIMALS

Every word listed is contained within the group of letters. Words can be found in a straight line horizontally, vertically, or diagonally. They may be read either forward or backward.

AUROCH

DINOSAUR

DIRE WOLF

EOHIPPUS

ICHTHYOSAUR

MAMMOTH

MASTODON

MEGATHERIUM

PLESIOSAUR

PTEROSAUR

QUAGGA

SMILODON

THYLACINE

TRILOBITE

T K U A N H B M T E F S E W W
M O P R O Y B S S W A Y T S R
U P S H D X S I T Z F Y I U U
I H L D O M X H T J L R B P A
R C C E T P Y L P S O T O P S
E O G L S L Q T G V W M L I O
H R V Y A I E D Z R E A I H N
T U A C M R O S K U R M R O I
A A I I O S M S U K I M T E D
G N M S X I Q D A E D O Z Y
E T A T L E U P V U F T A O V
M U V O S Q A L M J R H O G L
R I D P X M G M B A O O O M T
D O X K S K G M V Q T Y C Z R
N H Y R R U A S O Y H T H C I

171

PROPER NAME

Solve the puzzle using 6 remaining letters. HINT: Started as a contestant on FOX, ended as a judge on NBC.

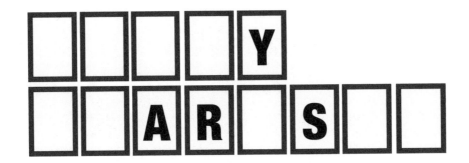

Answers on page 370.

ON THE MAP

Solve the puzzle using 4 remaining letters. HINT: In an Oscar nominated movie, Bruce Dern's character travels across state lines to claim a million-dollar marketing prize.

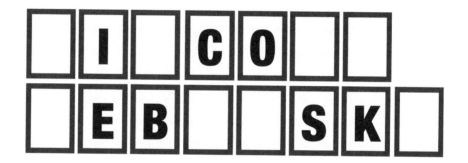

TREES

This puzzle follows the rules of your typical word search: Every variety of tree listed is contained within the group of letters. Words can be found in a straight line horizontally, vertically, or diagonally. They may read either forward or backward. But, in this version, words wrap up, down, and around the 3 sides of the cube.

AILANTHUS

APPLE

BREADFRUIT

BUCKEYE

CHESTNUT

CHINABERRY

EBONY

EUCALYPTUS

HAZEL

HEMLOCK

HICKORY

HOLLY

JUNIPER

KUMQUAT

LABURNUM

MAHOGANY

MAPLE

NUTMEG

OLIVE

PINE

PLUM

POMEGRANATE

SEQUOIA

SYCAMORE

TAMARIND

TULIP

WILLOW

Answers on page 370.

A CROSS EARTH

Complete the word search below to reveal a hidden message related to the puzzle's topic. Words can be found in a straight line horizontally, vertically, or diagonally. They may read either forward or backward. Once you find all the words, you can read the hidden message from the remaining letters, top to bottom, left to right.

AGRA (India)
APIA (Samoa)
ASPEN (Colorado)
ATLANTA (Georgia)
BALI (Indonesia)
BATH (England)
BERLIN (Germany)
BERN (Switzerland)
BOGOTA (Colombia)
BOISE (Idaho)
BONN (Germany)
BOSTON (Massachusetts)
BREST (France)
BUTTE (Montana)
CALI (Colombia)
CHAD (Africa)
CHICAGO (Illinois)
CORK (Ireland)
DALLAS (Texas)
GENOA (Italy)
GRAZ (Austria)

HOUSTON (Texas)
HOVE (England)
INDIANAPOLIS (Indiana)
JACKSON (Mississippi)
JENA (Germany)
JUNEAU (Alaska)
LAOS (Asia)
LAREDO (Texas)
LIEGE (Belgium)
LIMA (Peru)
LINCOLN (Nebraska)
LODI (New Jersey)
LOME (Togo)
MACON (Georgia)
MAN (Island)
MECCA (Saudi Arabia)
MESA (Arizona)
METZ (France)
MILAN (Italy)
MINNEAPOLIS (Minnesota)
MUMBAI (India)

NEW ORLEANS (Louisiana)
NEW YORK (New York)
NICE (France)
OHIO (USA)
OSLO (Norway)
PARA (Brazil)
PERTH (Australia)
PERU (South America)
PORTLAND (Oregon)
QUITO (Ecuador)
RABAT (Morocco)
RENO (Nevada)

RIGA (Latvia)
ROME (Italy)
ST. PETERSBURG (Florida)
SAN ANTONIO (Texas)
SAN FRANCISCO (California)
SANTA FE (New Mexico)
SEATTLE (Washington)
SELMA (Alabama)
SPOKANE (Washington)
TALLAHASSEE (Florida)
TALLINN (Estonia)

LEFTOVER LETTERS SPELL A RELATED NAME (2 WORDS):

```
A N E J M                              O H I O S
R Z D U E Z S                       H I B U T T E
G A T N A L T A                   O N O O A P I A
A R B E A S P E N                 U O I T S E R B M
  G D A L L A S M F             S T S A N T A F E
    I U T O T I U Q R       T N E M I E O O S
      R O D E R A L D A S O A L U C R N N A
        S I L O P A E N N I M E S E E
        U R E P N O A C B S B G R
          A E A S S A I U J
          W R S T I L R S A
        L O I T A S O G O N C C M
      O R D A H C P A G T R K O N A
    S M L S E L M A M E H O E S R S I N R
  M E E G E I L N I       A B O K R P L B O
  O G A C I H C A L         L N E W Y O R K M
B B N T C A L I R             L A N N C K E E E
A S A T A O D A               A N N N S A B E
T A L L I N N                   T M I L A N A
H O V E I                         L O D I E
```

THINGS

Solve the puzzle using 6 remaining letters. HINT: The memories we don't forget.

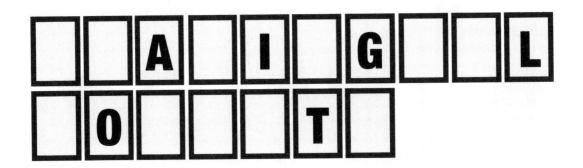

Answers on page 370.

WHAT ARE YOU WEARING?

Solve the puzzle using 6 remaining letters. HINT: You probably won't let anyone borrow this.

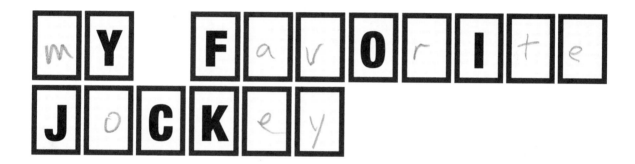

MY FAVORITE

JOCKEY

Answers on page 370.

ELEVATOR WORDS

Like an elevator, words move up and down the "floors" of this puzzle. Starting with the first answer, the second part of each answer carries down to become the first part of the following answer. With the clues given, complete the puzzle.

1. Get in _touch_   1. Establish communications

2. _____ _____   2. Judging criterion

3. _____ _____   3. Absolutely

4. _Cold_ _feet_   4. Strong apprehension

5. _Feet_ _first_   5. Safer way to jump in

6. _First_ _ladies_   6. Abigail Adams and Martha Washington

7. _Ladies_ night   7. An occasion where women get discounts

Answers on page 370.

RHYME TIME

Solve the puzzle using 3 remaining letters. HINT: Where'd you get those peepers?

WHY WEIGHT?

Homophones are words that sound the same but are spelled differently and have different meanings (in the title of this puzzle, for example, "wait" should actually be used instead of "weight"). To complete this puzzle, first fill in the homophone(s) for each word listed below. Then, find both the original word and its homophone (s) in the grid. Words can be found vertically, horizontally, or diagonally, and may read forward or backward.

1. ADDITION _____
2. ALLOWED _____
3. ASCENT _____
4. AWFUL _____
5. BILLED _____
6. BRAID _____
7. CACHE _____
8. CAPITAL _____
9. CREWED _____
10. CUE _____
11. DISCREET _____
12. FAZE _____
13. GAMBLE _____
14. GORED _____
15. HEARD _____

16. KERNEL _____
17. LAIR _____
18. LEASED _____
19. MANNER _____
20. MUSTARD _____
21. PARISH _____
22. PHLOX _____
23. PRINCIPAL _____
24. STATIONARY _____

Bonus (find two homophones for each):

25. EWES _____ _____
26. PEAK _____ _____
27. RAYS _____ _____

```
D E W O L L A S C E N T E S Y A R
A N U L O B M A G J U Y U B H E H
S T E E R C S I D F L O C K S U R
W T C T P H S I R E P F N D I Q T
D R A T S U M S N M Y F T L R I S
E Q P T D V L O T I P A C I A P A
W M I X I N L Y P L D L R U P L E
E U T O R O N A M F R K M B O S L
R S A L C D N X C N U P Z U A T H
C T L H Q T P A O U O R D H L A G
X E L P I C N I R P G I P C U T D
S R E X L C T E V Y S N T S B I E
D E D A Q I F H S C E C E I D O L
K D Y E D U R C R S Z I G E D N L
K E L D R Y E E L D A P S P T E I
R Q A E E O T U R W R A D I A R B
T Y Z W N E G A E B E L W S H Y I
Y A S Y D R E H W L A I R F E R L
F B C A C H E B R E N N A M U W B
D E S I A R N K A E P G A M B L E
```

Answers on page 371.

WHAT ARE YOU DOING?

Solve the puzzle using 8 remaining letters. HINT: You're going to need this before you go swimming.

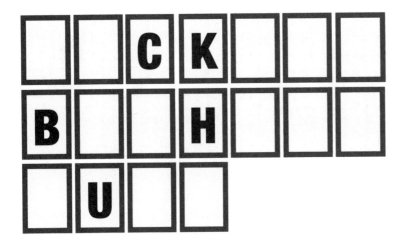

Answers on page 371.

ON THE MAP

Solve the puzzle using 7 remaining letters. HINT: Stop to see Sedona on this route.

Answers on page 371.

RHYME TIME

Solve the puzzle using 4 remaining letters. HINT: This marsupial is very keen.

Answers on page 371.

RHYME TIME

Each clue leads to a 2-word answer that rhymes, such as BIG PIG or STABLE TABLE. The numbers in parentheses after the clue give the number of letters in each word. For example, "cookware taken from the oven (3, 3)" would be "hot pot." As a bonus, figure out what the answers have in common.

1. Bronx animal attraction got bigger (3, 4):

2. Was acquainted with baseball great Gehrig (4, 3):

3. Hurled a loafer (5, 4):

4. Look at what Dr. Seuss's Horton heard (4, 3):

5. Smote a wildebeest (4, 3):

RHYME TIME

Solve the puzzle using 4 remaining letters. HINT: It's also the name of a charity that helps job seekers.

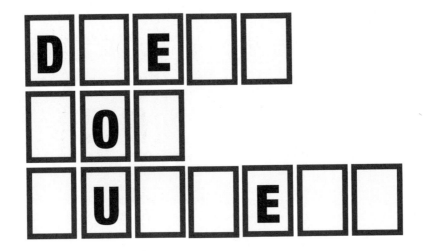

Answers on page 371.

FUN & GAMES

Solve the puzzle using 4 remaining letters. HINT: Right before Allie and Noah share a kiss in *The Notebook*.

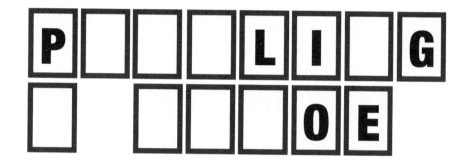

P _ _ _ L I _ G

_ _ _ _ O E

EVENT

Solve the puzzle using 5 remaining letters. HINT: A media event often held by politicians, sports teams, and celebrities.

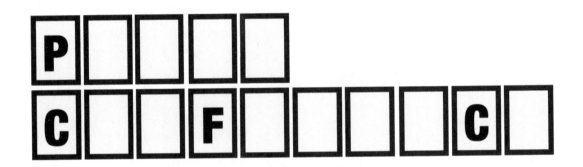

RHYME TIME

Solve the puzzle using 3 remaining letters. HINT: A flashy show.

R _ _ _ L E -
_ _ _ _ L E

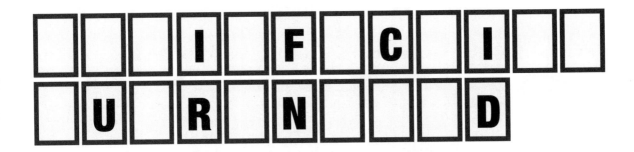

PHRASE

Solve the puzzle using 7 remaining letters. HINT: As hard as The Rolling Stones tried, they couldn't get it.

| | | | I | | F | | C | | I | | |
| | U | | R | | N | | | | D | |

Answers on page 371.

LIVING THING

Solve the puzzle using 6 remaining letters. HINT: Bears a strong resemblance to a direwolf on *Game of Thrones*.

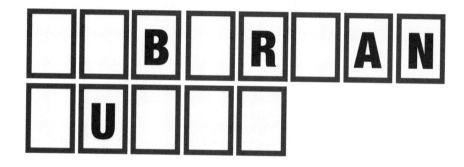

Answers on page 371.

PHRASE

Solve the puzzle using 6 remaining letters. HINT: Are you sure you want to wake up?

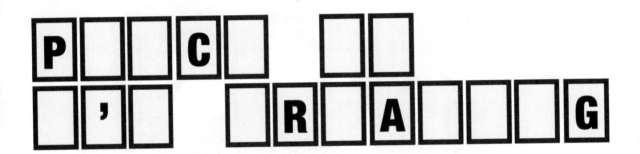

Answers on page 371.

THING

Solve the puzzle using 5 remaining letters. HINT: Vincent van Gogh only sold one piece while he was alive; however, now his art is no longer for sale.

	R		C		L		
	A		T			G	

BEFORE & AFTER

Solve the puzzle using 6 remaining letters. HINT: Engine is a noun.

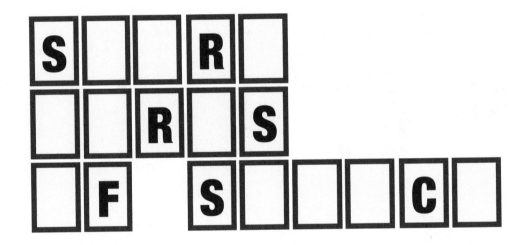

Answers on page 371.

SHOW BIZ

Solve the puzzle using 5 remaining letters. HINT: To ensure this happens make the audience get up before you perform.

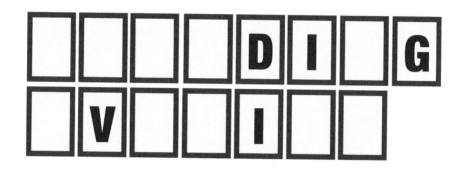

Answers on page 371.

TITLE & AUTHOR

Solve the puzzle using 7 remaining letters. HINT: Reader, I married him . . . eventually.

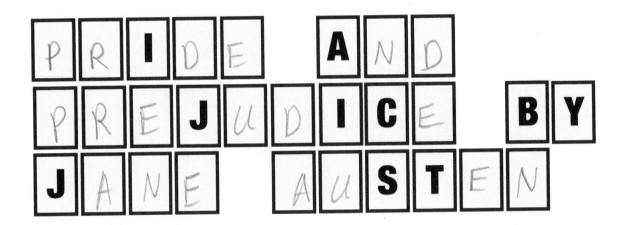

PRIDE AND
PREJUDICE BY
JANE AUSTEN

Answers on page 371.

WORD LADDERS

Change just one letter on each line to go from the top word to the bottom word. Do not change the order of the letters. You must have a common English word at each step.

1. RHYME

—————

—————— an Oxfordshire town

—————

Shake Bond preferred it if the bartender did this to his martini

—————

—————

STALL

---

2. GRIME

—————

—————

—————— thick and messy liquid

—————

—————

—————

SWIPE

Answers on page 372.

PLACES

Solve the puzzle using 5 remaining letters. HINT: Cinque Terre is known for its beautiful union of land and sea.

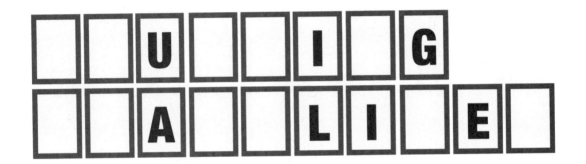

Answers on page 372.

ON THE MAP

Solve the puzzle using 7 remaining letters. HINT: It's always best to stay neutral.

RHYME TIME

Each clue leads to a 2-word answer that rhymes, such as BIG PIG or STABLE TABLE. The numbers in parentheses after the clue give the number of letters in each word. For example, "cookware taken from the oven (3, 3)" would be "hot pot."

1. Equal portion (4, 5):

2. Hip place to go to class (4, 6):

3. Zoom by (5, 4):

4. Tidy high schooler (5, 4):

5. Light bite for a group of wolves (4, 5):

6. Seat with no rounded edges (6, 5):

7. Young cow's chuckles (5, 6):

8. Nicer restaurant (5, 5):

9. Crazy chocolate (4, 5):

10. One who cuts the grass with less haste (6, 5):

11. Took black chunks from a mine (5, 4):

Answers on page 372.

ELEVATOR WORDS

Like an elevator, words move up and down the "floors" of this puzzle. Starting with the first answer, the second part of each answer carries down to become the first part of the following answer. With the clues given, complete the puzzle.

1. Day_____

2. _____ _____

3. _____ _____

4. _____ _____

5. _____ _____

6. _____

7. _____ fluid

1. Dawn

2. Crack, as a coconut

3. Magic access phrase

4. TV show for tots

5. It helps illuminate the way

6. Municipal employee of the past

7. Fuel of sorts

Answers on page 372.

RHYME TIME

Solve the puzzle using 5 remaining letters. HINT: Like an electrical transformer?

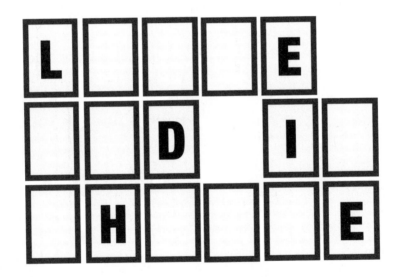

Answers on page 372.

BEFORE & AFTER

Use the letters below to fill in the boxes and reveal the 2 related words. Connected boxes share the same letter.

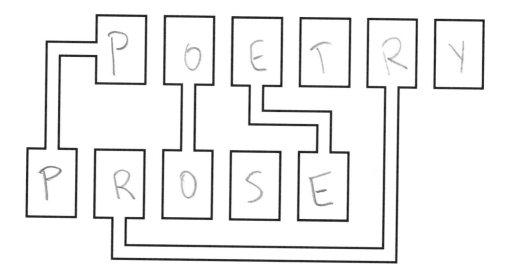

EOPRSTY

CODE-DOKU

Solve this puzzle just as you would a sudoku. Use deductive logic to complete the grid so that each row, column, and 3 by 3 box contains the letters from the word DAUGHTERS.

	A	R						
	U						H	S
			U	H				A
	R			S				D
U		T				S		G
G			E				R	
R			H	E				
A	E						U	
						E	D	

Answers on page 372.

LIVING THING

Solve the puzzle using 7 remaining letters. HINT: This sidekick wants to know when you're *leaving Cheyenne*.

DOGS OF TV & MOVIES

Every word listed is contained within the group of letters. Words can be found in a straight line horizontally, vertically, or diagonally. They may be read either forward or backward.

AIRBUD

ASTRO

BENJI

BLUE

CLIFFORD

EDDIE

FRED BASSET

GOOFY

HOOCH

LADY

LASSIE

MARLEY

MARMADUKE

NANA

ODIE

OLD YELLER

PLUTO

SCOOBY DOO

SKIP

SNOOPY

TOTO

TRAMP

UNDERDOG

208

```
R  S  O  Z  L  X  R  A  A  O  R  T  S  A  M
T  T  D  A  H  Y  V  D  T  C  R  Q  L  Z  K
E  S  D  E  X  E  M  A  R  M  A  D  U  K  E
S  Y  X  U  O  L  G  X  Z  O  H  A  G  P  A
S  P  Z  L  Q  R  R  O  X  O  F  Y  L  N  H
A  Q  L  B  E  A  E  E  O  F  P  F  A  G  R
B  G  V  U  D  M  Q  C  L  O  M  N  I  B  T
D  T  O  X  T  V  H  P  O  L  G  J  N  L  P
E  F  R  D  M  O  Z  N  U  V  E  K  V  M  C
R  Y  C  A  R  D  S  C  O  O  B  Y  D  O  O
F  T  F  I  M  E  U  E  O  C  X  E  D  F  E
T  E  T  O  I  P  D  B  X  T  C  Q  N  L  G
H  E  I  D  O  Y  I  N  R  H  O  D  V  J  O
L  E  D  P  N  G  R  K  U  I  Q  T  B  F  I
S  E  I  S  S  A  L  K  S  U  A  J  L  J  T
```

LIVING THING

Solve the puzzle using 6 remaining letters. HINT: Large, padded feet help this endangered beauty climb mountains.

Answers on page 372.

BIG TOP CODE-DOKU

Solve this puzzle just as you would a sudoku. Use deductive logic to complete the grid so that each row, each column, and each 3 by 3 box contains each of the letters in the anagram IT'S NO MEAL in some order. The solution is unique. When you have completed the puzzle, read the shaded squares from left to right and top to bottom to reveal a phrase describing something you might see at the circus.

Hidden message:

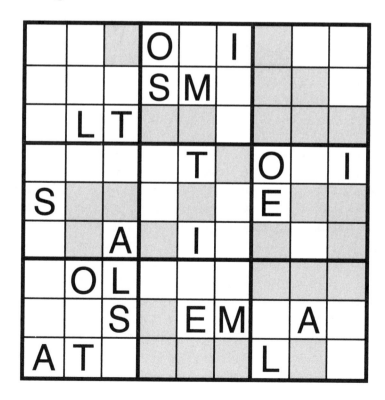

EVENT

Solve the puzzle using 5 remaining letters. HINT: Slow and steady wins the race.

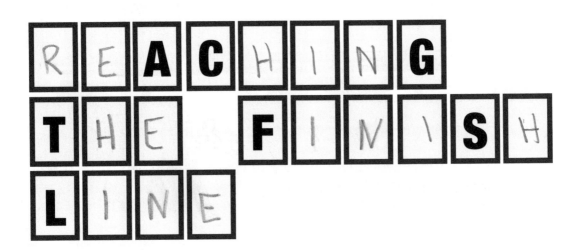

REACHING
THE FINISH
LINE

Answers on page 373.

ON THE MAP

Solve the puzzle using 5 remaining letters. HINT: Home of the Grey Sloan hospital.

Answers on page 373.

MOVIE TITLE

Solve the puzzle using 4 remaining letters. HINT: I'm the Dude.

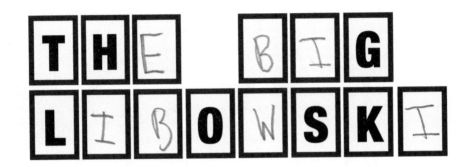

ON THE MAP

Solve the puzzle using 5 remaining letters. HINT: 1/3 of the Pacific Crest Trail.

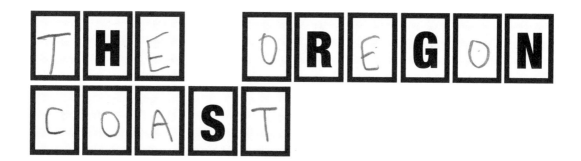

THE OREGON
COAST

Answers on page 373.

LIVING THING

Solve the puzzle using 7 remaining letters. HINT: Its energy stems from predation.

P _ _ _ _ _ R
P L _ _ _

Answers on page 373.

FOR THE BIRDS

Place each bird into the grid. There are some letters already in place to get you flying.

3 Letters

Owl

4 Letters

Dove

Lark

5 Letters

Eagle

Goose

Robin

6 Letters

Pigeon

8 Letters

Bluebird

Parakeet

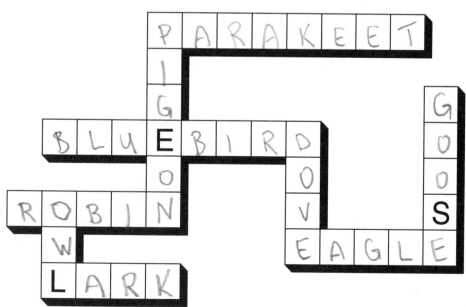

Answers on page 373.

CROSSWORD

ACROSS

1. Ella Fitzgerald specialty
5. Single-celled critter
10. Brother of Jacob
14. Ear part
15. Grief, in poetry
16. Pass over
17. Surrounding glow
18. Map within a map
19. Lancelot and Mix-a-Lot, for two
20. Bird who thinks he's Louis Armstrong?
23. Clairvoyant's gift
24. Regret
25. Sea serpent slain by Hercules
28. So out it's in
30. Verve
33. Grab a bite
34. Grown-up doodlebug
37. Trait carrier
38. Fish with an inflated ego?
40. Bearing
42. Let go
43. "Black gold"
44. White-hot anger
45. Cleaned the floor
49. Garlicky sauce
51. Where Springsteen was born, in song
53. Dove's call
54. Tree that's oh so sad?
59. "Don't preach," Madonna told him
61. "Hello" singer
62. Easily maneuvered, as a ship
63. Bacteria culture medium
64. High-altitude nest
65. Cambodian dollar
66. No longer new
67. Hen's perch
68. Blows it

DOWN

1. Christian of "Windtalkers"
2. Dinner portion
3. Short, but not necessarily sweet
4. Sports side
5. "Au revoir!"
6. Carlo or Cristo lead-in
7. Alternative word
8. Certain Afrikaner
9. Music and dance, e.g.
10. "How I Spent My Summer," often
11. Superficial, as beauty
12. Chest filler
13. Emotional peaks
21. Antler point
22. Doctor from the planet Gallifrey
26. Competed in a 10K
27. Absorbed, as costs
29. "___ Man" (Hoffman title role)
30. Oniony breakfast roll
31. Took a bus, say
32. Ancient Peruvian

218

35. By way of, for short
36. Wolf's look
37. Filled out
38. Like an eagle, e.g.
39. Very quick, musically
40. Bygone bird of New Zealand
41. 3, on sundials
44. Old expression of distaste
46. Cousin of a napoleon
47. More needy

48. Locker room stack
50. Live and ____
51. Wrinkly citrus fruits
52. Like Georgia Brown
55. "The Tonight Show" host, once
56. Prefix with gram or logical
57. Infamous Roman fiddler
58. Ancient harp
59. A dog extends it to "shake"
60. Give it ____ (try)

Answers on page 373.

ON THE MAP

Solve the puzzle using 8 remaining letters. HINT: This feature of the Indian subcontinent is the largest of its kind in the world.

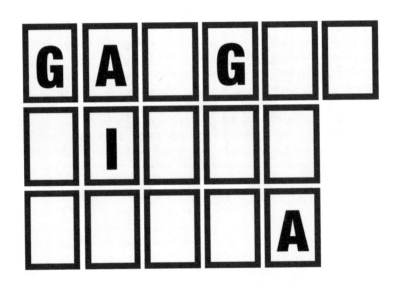

Answers on page 373.

PEOPLE

Solve the puzzle using 6 remaining letters. HINT: A pair of siblings.

VITAL SIGN

Travel in sequence through the puzzle from the left side to the right, using each numbered clue to determine the correct word. Connect adjacent words with a common letter to proceed through the maze. Some letters are already given. The first and last words tie into the title.

1. Vampire snack

2. Dent

3. Glimmer

4. First president

5. From dusk on

6. Relate

7. Joke response

8. Place to eat

9. To drive down

10. Like 2 peas in a _____

11. Cloudy, wet, and cold

12. 365 days

13. Allotment

14. Most loud

15. Canvas cover

16. Support

17. Urge

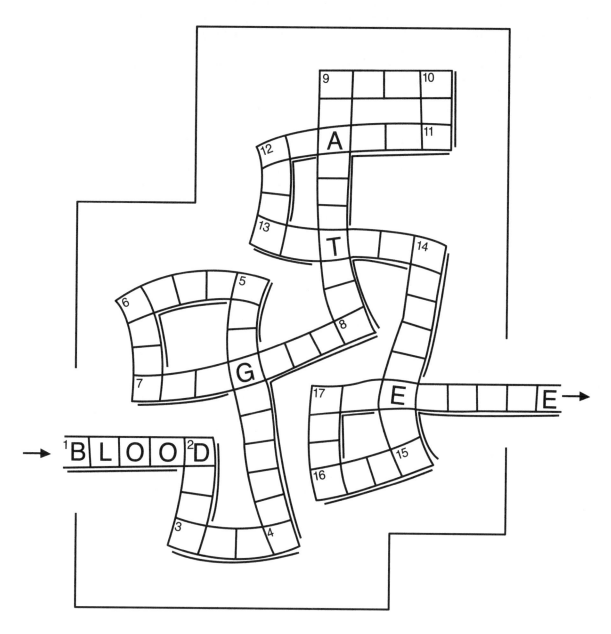

FOOD & DRINK

Solve the puzzle using 5 remaining letters. HINT: tangy seafood dessert.

LIVING THINGS

Solve the puzzle using 4 remaining letters. HINT: Grab your snorkeling gear and begin exploring.

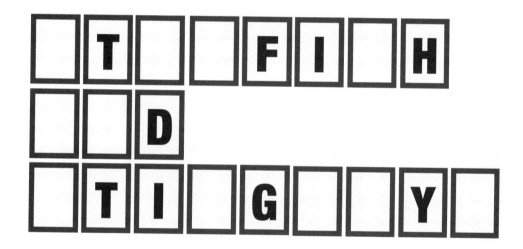

HORSE BREEDS

Every word listed below is contained within the group of letters. Words can be found in a straight line horizontally, vertically, or diagonally. They may read either forward or backward.

ABYSSINIAN

APPALOOSA

ARABIAN

ASTURIAN

AZTECA

BELGIAN

BUCKSKIN

CARTHUSIAN

CASPIAN

CLYDESDALE

DALES PONY

GELDERLANDER

HIGHLAND PONY

MINIATURE

MUSTANG

PALOMINO

PINTO

QUARTER HORSE

```
H K N L P A L O M I N O N V Q
I T T G E L D E R L A N D E R
G A E S R O H R E T R A U Q T
H M S F J W N I K S K C U B C
L A B T M U S T A N G N M L A
A Z R T U N Z L V N D A E T R
N T T N D R B N A T A I L N T
D E N Q A E I S W L L N A C H
P C Z M L I O A Z R E I D Q U
O A B G M O P R N M S S S Y S
N K I T L W C S X P P S E G I
Y A R A B I A N A X O Y D R A
N T P J Y G J K K C N B Y G N
K P P I N T O M T B Y A L Q N
A E R U T A I N I M L J C T K
```

LIVING THING

Solve the puzzle using 7 remaining letters. HINT: The most famous of these is Rocket J.

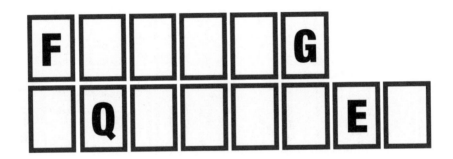

Answers on page 374.

ON THE MAP

Solve the puzzle using 6 remaining letters. HINT: There are no broken dreams on this road.

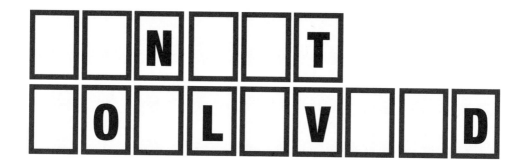

Answers on page 374.

STAR & ROLE

Solve the puzzle using 5 remaining letters. HINT: The *nom de guerre* of Steve Rogers.

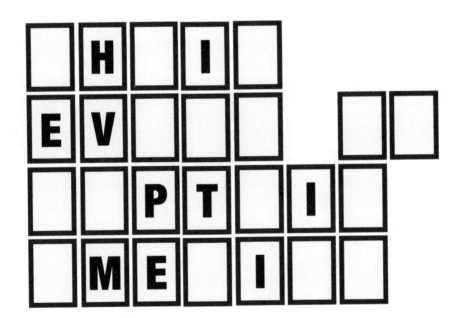

Answers on page 374.

THE SILENT TYPE

Change just one letter on each line to go from the top word to the bottom word. Do not change the order of the letters. You must have a common English word or a name at each step.

LIAM

_____

_____ Shakespearean king

_____

_____

_____

LIST

PHRASE

Solve the puzzle using 6 remaining letters. HINT: Look to the galaxy for your good fortune.

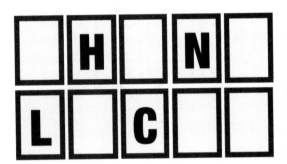

Answers on page 374.

LANDMARK

Solve the puzzle using 5 remaining letters. HINT: The Iron Lady of Paris.

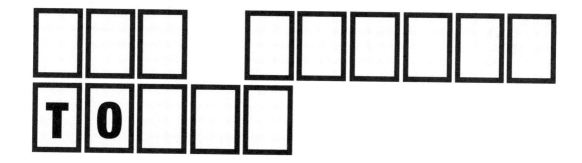

ELEVATOR WORDS

Like an elevator, words move up and down the "floors" of this puzzle. Starting with the first answer, the second part of each answer carries down to become the first part of the following answer. With the clues given, complete the puzzle.

1. Passion _____

2. _____ _____

3. _____ _____

4. _____ _____

5. _____ _____

6. _____ _____

7. _____ curtain

1. Sherbet ingredient

2. Light appetizer

3. Party garment

4. Preparation before the first performance

5. Prewedding custom

6. It provides a full evening of entertainment

7. This is raised to start the show

Answers on page 374.

STAR & ROLE

Solve the puzzle using 7 remaining letters. HINT: Both leads won acting Oscars and the film won five in total.

PHRASE

Solve the puzzle using 5 remaining letters. HINT: Part of a much bigger problem.

Answers on page 374.

PHRASE

Solve the puzzle using 7 remaining letters. HINT: If you don't know all the facts but believe it to be true.

Answers on page 374.

CLASSIC WESTERN

Every word listed is contained within the group of letters. Words can be found in a straight line horizontally, vertically, or diagonally. They may be read either forward or backward.

AMBUSH	PONIES
BULLETS	PRAIRIE
CACTUS	RANCH
CANYON	RIDER
CATTLE	SADDLE
CORRAL	SAGEBRUSH
COWBOY	SALOON
COYOTE	SHERIFF
DEPUTY	SHOTGUN
DRAW	SOMBRERO
GUNFIGHT	SUNSET
HOLSTER	TRAIL
OUTLAW	WAGON
PARTNER	WANTED
PINTO	WHISKEY

```
M  F  N  U  G  T  O  H  S  S  Q  L  K  O  H  E  C
H  S  U  B  M  A  C  C  T  F  E  I  Y  C  G  Z  A
O  W  C  R  C  O  H  E  J  X  D  A  G  A  S  K  W
I  Z  Z  O  W  K  L  X  S  Y  V  R  V  Z  O  T  S
N  T  U  B  Y  L  Z  B  L  G  P  T  P  Y  M  X  G
Y  O  O  I  U  O  A  L  A  R  R  O  C  D  B  T  R
E  Y  Y  B  O  U  T  L  A  W  E  A  N  R  R  B  K
K  J  U  N  C  L  V  E  C  S  A  D  D  L  E  K  Y
S  R  K  A  A  G  D  A  P  H  J  N  I  Y  R  N  N
I  Y  U  T  J  C  T  D  R  G  C  D  O  R  O  O  J
H  K  M  X  H  T  Z  E  A  U  P  N  G  O  G  C  U
W  X  U  P  L  U  A  T  I  N  Z  X  A  A  L  H  A
U  H  D  E  Q  D  D  N  R  F  S  F  W  R  H  A  R
G  K  Z  V  D  T  Z  A  I  I  J  M  C  F  D  E  S
P  A  R  T  N  E  R  W  E  G  R  K  F  V  T  Q  P
O  T  N  I  P  R  P  F  A  H  P  I  P  S  B  J  Z
X  S  U  N  S  E  T  U  V  T  R  P  L  C  G  P  W
W  A  R  D  B  O  V  F  T  E  Y  O  X  F  F  K  C
S  A  G  E  B  R  U  S  H  Y  H  S  E  I  N  O  P
G  C  B  P  B  A  H  S  U  T  C  A  C  N  S  J  Y
```

Answers on page 374.

239

CROSSWORD

ACROSS

1. Sister's garb
6. Address for the king
10. Chinese gemstone
14. Alpha's opposite
15. Singles
16. Sleeping, say
17. Male star who likes collecting Barbie dolls
19. Glob on a potter's wheel
20. "Is it a boy ___ girl?"
21. Camping stuff
22. Leaf gatherers
24. Sunday speech
26. Coin toss option
28. Abbr. on a cornerstone
30. Shangri-la and Avalon, e.g.
34. Lion's "meow"
37. NASA go-aheads
39. "___ la vista, baby"
40. Roast beef chain
42. "___ for Ricochet" (Grafton)
43. First sign of the zodiac
44. Commandments verb
45. Bearded flower
47. Highways: Abbr.
48. Public image
50. Canyon sound
52. It's tougher than string
54. "What a pity!"
58. Oscar winner as Queen Elizabeth
61. Croquet field
63. Opposite of sing.
64. Aunt Bee raised him
65. Well-known role for 25-Down

68. Prefix meaning "bone"
69. Affirm as true
70. Trigger, for one
71. Lather (up)
72. Word with "souci" or "serif"
73. Crossword cookies

DOWN

1. Orange-roofed restaurants, for short
2. "...like a big pizza pie, that's ___"
3. "The View" co-host Joy
4. Car key's place: Abbr.
5. Dances for two
6. Cola or ginger ale
7. Like argon or helium
8. Agent, briefly
9. Liveliness
10. Well-known role for 17-Across
11. Competent, like a seaman
12. Diary opener
13. One of its flavors is Turtle Sundae
18. Matchmaker in "Fiddler"
23. "Welcome" in Waikiki
25. Star who played 65-Across
27. Shrimp-on-the-barbie eater
29. "The Picture of ___ Gray"
31. "What time ___?"
32. Words after suit to or fit to
33. Be cheeky with
34. Feature of husky voices
35. "What's Hecuba to him ___ to Hecuba": Hamlet
36. "This duck walks into ___"
38. Cassis apéritif
41. "Uncle Tom's Cabin" author
46. "Uh" sound
49. Fictional teenage turtles
51. Big kahuna

53. Show host DeGeneres
55. Chapel topper
56. "This is ___ sudden!"
57. Guys, these days
58. Calls from Bossy

59. ___ facto
60. Beatles meter maid
62. Breeze-dries
66. Charlottesville sch.
67. Vert. opposite

STAR & ROLE

Solve the puzzle using 7 remaining letters. HINT: His English accent is never explained.

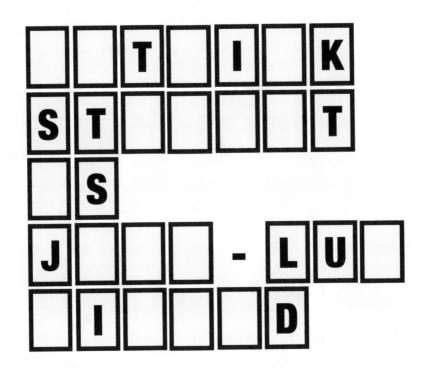

MISS FAYE

Change just one letter on each line to go from the top word to the bottom word. Do not change the order of the letters. You must have a common English word or a name at each step.

FAYE

_____ zany Martha

_____

_____ Campanella and Clark

_____ Aussie hoppers

_____

_____

_____

JOAN

OSCAR WINNING MOVIES

Time for some Hollywood history! We've described 15 "Best Picture" Oscar winners below. How many you can fill in? Words can be found in a straight line horizontally, vertically, or diagonally. They may read either forward or backward.

1. This 1972 mobster flick was directed by Francis Ford Coppola and won Best Picture. It spawned 2 sequels, one of which also won the Best Picture award.

2. Ron Howard directed Russell Crowe and Jennifer Connelly in this 2001 best-picture winner about the mathematician John Nash.

3. This 1985 film by Sydney Pollack starred Robert Redford and Meryl Streep and was set largely in Kenya and surrounding areas.

4. Starring Tom Cruise and Dustin Hoffman, this film about an autistic savant won 4 Oscars in 1989, including Best Picture.

5. This 1984 biopic was loosely based on a supposed eighteenth century rivalry between Wolfgang Mozart and Antonio Salieri.

6. This 1969 drama starred Jon Voight as a fish-out-of-water Texan trying to make it in New York City.

7. Often ranked as one of the greatest films of all time, this 1942 romantic drama starred Humphrey Bogart and Ingrid Bergman and was set in World War II Morocco.

8. This 1970 war biopic starred George C. Scott as the title character. The opening monologue, with Scott giving a speech in front of an enormous American flag, is one of the most iconic images in all of film history.

9. Audrey Hepburn and Rex Harrison starred in this 1964 musical about a Cockney-accented flower girl named Eliza Doolittle.

10. Directed and produced by Clint Eastwood and with him in the starring role as gunslinger William Munny, this 1992 film was only the third western ever to win for Best Picture.

11. This quirky 1994 comedy-drama starred Tom Hanks and included such famous lines as "stupid is as stupid does" and "life is like a box of chocolates."

12. This 1976 boxing flick starring Sylvester Stallone spawned 6 sequels.

13. This 1997 film by James Cameron starred Leonardo DiCaprio and Kate Winslet, and was the highest-grossing film of all time... until it was beaten by Cameron's 3-D blockbuster "Avatar" in 2010.

14. Mel Gibson directed and starred in this 1995 historical epic about the 13th century Scottish hero William Wallace.

15. This 2002 film starring Renee Zellweger, Catherine Zeta-Jones, and Richard Gere was the first musical to win Best Picture since 1968.

```
C M I D N I G H T C O W B O Y
F H U N F O R G I V E N A V A
J F I L O U L I Z T D C D K B
P Y J C C P L L O R N I G G E
R M O Z A X Y C Q A S Y I Y A
A Y U K W G J Z L E M X F C U
I D M G O L O B H H M P I A T
N A Z C T N A D G E Q R R M I
M L T F O S T S F V F A S A F
A R I T A A E Q N A M U B D U
N I T C D N R R F R T I J E L
I A A M T J T O R B O H X U M
P F N A N L T H C O Z K E S I
Q Y I R W U R S C K F U S R N
B M C X O L V K U Q Y O Z V D
```

WHAT ARE YOU DOING?

Solve the puzzle using 5 remaining letters. HINT: It can be hard to fall asleep at night.

Answers on page 375.

FUN & GAMES

Solve the puzzle using 6 remaining letters. HINT: Sailing without a boat.

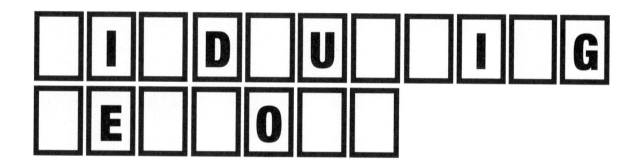

VOWELLESS TV
& MOVIE GUIDE

To cut down on printing costs and make more room for the growing number of TV programs and movies available to the public, the publishers of the *Weekly Guide to Entertainment* have decided to print all the program titles without vowels. Listed below are the titles of 20 classic movies and TV programs written with the new system. Can you figure them out before next week's edition comes out?

TV SHOWS

1. BNNZ
2. BNSN
3. DLLS
4. FRDS
5. GNSMK
6. JFFRSNS
7. LC
8. QNC
9. TX
10. TMRRW

MOVIES

1. CDDSHCK
2. CNDRLL
3. GRS
4. JWS
5. LN
6. MTBLLS
7. RCK
8. RPLN
9. RTHQK
10. SPRMN

248

Answers on page 375.

DIAMOND CUT

Follow the arrows to solve each clue and complete the grid.

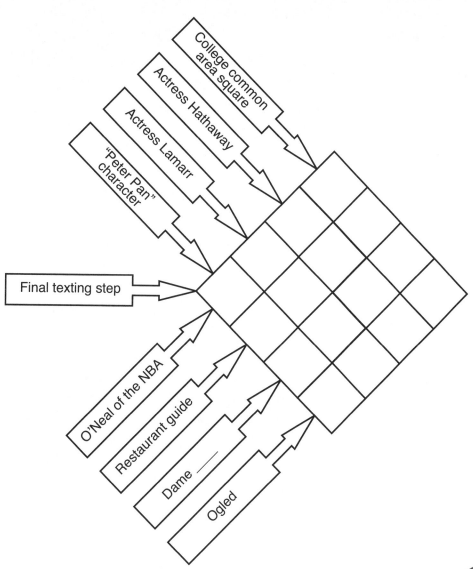

Clues:
- College common area square
- Actress Hathaway
- Actress Lamarr
- "Peter Pan" character
- Final texting step
- O'Neal of the NBA
- Restaurant guide
- Dame _____
- Ogled

Answers on page 376.

3 FOR 2

That is, 3 letters for 2 answers! Here's how it works: We provide 3 letters and a category, and you come up with 2 answers from that category in which the 3 letters appear in the same sequence. Example: If the category is SIGNS OF THE ZODIAC, and we gave you the 3 letters COR, your answers would be SCORPIO and CAPRICORN. Or if we had given you the letters ARI in the same category, you could have chosen 2 signs from AQUARIUS, SAGITTARIUS or ARIES.

1. CAR Vegetables_____

2. ERI Great Lakes_____

3. EMB Months _____

4. HAR Deserts _____

5. GAR European countries_____

250

Answers on page 376.

ON THE MAP

Solve the puzzle using 5 remaining letters. HINT: This diverse Gulf city is a popular spring-break destination.

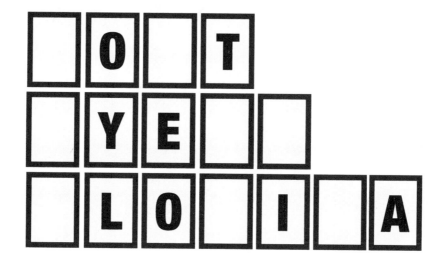

CROSSWORD

ACROSS
1. "Lady" of pop
5. Calvary letters
9. Compete on ice
14. "When I Was ___" ("HMS Pin afore" song)
15. Mark Harmon TV series
16. Breaking a bad one is good
17. Came home feet first
18. Disney lion queen
19. "I Once Loved ___" (folk song)
20. USA's largest capital city and its state
23. 1926 Channel swimmer
24. Druggist, to Brits
28. Artist Gerard ___ Borch
29. Common bonds?
32. Neptune's neighbor
33. Confer holy orders on
35. "Nana" author Émile
36. This started out as Fort Raccoon
40. Certain Ford, for short
41. Japanese port near Nagasaki
42. Start back up again
45. "So that's how it is"
46. One who plays for pay
49. Poetic "soon"
51. Arabic for "peace"
53. Capital city with America's oldest wooden fort

56. Hit play shortage
59. "Got milk?" sound?
60. Miss, in Mexico: Abbr.
61. April Fools' Day sign
62. ___ noire (pet peeve)
63. One who usually has a ball?
64. No longer trendy
65. Newspaper opinion piece
66. Icelandic epic

DOWN
1. Pilot light, e.g.
2. Refer casually (to)
3. Full ___ (dive)
4. Summer at the office
5. Subtle implication
6. College hoops org.
7. Small creek
8. Sci-fi author Asimov
9. Dinner table item
10. City where "I've got a gal," in song
11. Org. for Perry Mason
12. 1999 Frank McCourt book
13. Little green men, for short
21. Firehouse sound
22. Moo ___ pork
25. "___ pronounce you..."
26. 1973 Toni Morrison title
27. Airport screener's org.
30. Lecture platform
31. Mideast's ___ Peninsula
33. Kisses, fancily
34. Capone pursuer

36. Animal on road signs
37. Celtic language
38. Was wishy-washy
39. Steel girder
40. G.I. chow in Desert Storm
43. Dessert choice
44. College dept.
46. Like socks in a drawer
47. Spouted off

48. Pro golfer Mark
50. Okra stew
52. "Chocolat" director Hallstrom
54. Creep through the cracks
55. Farmer's market bag
56. It runs in the woods
57. The Gay Nineties, e.g.
58. Grafton's "___ for Alibi"

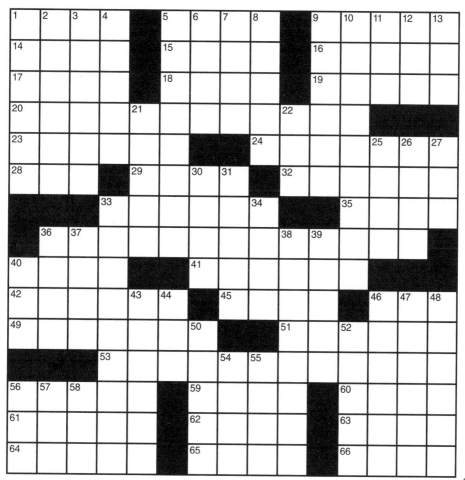

Answers on page 376.

TWO OF A KIND

Change just one letter on each line to go from the top word to the bottom word. Do not change the order of the letters. You must have a common English word or a name at each step.

OWEN

‾‾‾‾‾

‾‾‾‾‾

‾‾‾‾‾

‾‾‾‾‾

‾‾‾‾‾

‾‾‾‾‾

‾‾‾‾‾

LUKE

Answers on page 376.

STAR & ROLE

Solve the puzzle using 7 remaining letters. HINT: These films have earned nearly $3 billion in worldwide box office.

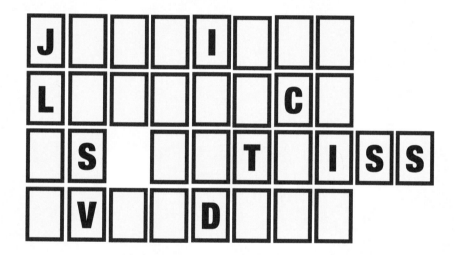

Answers on page 376.

OSCAR WINNING MOVIES

Figure out the full name of each actor or actress who played a starring role in all of the 3 films listed in each clue. Words can be found in a straight line horizontally, vertically, or diagonally. They may read either forward or backward.

1. Zoolander, Tropic Thunder, Meet the Parents: _____

2. To Die For, Moulin Rouge, The Others: _____

3. Erin Brockovich, Mystic Pizza, My Best Friend's Wedding: _____

4. Independence Day, Hancock, Men in Black: _____

5. Ace Ventura: Pet Detective, The Truman Show, Liar Liar: _____

6. Legends of the Fall, Fight Club, Troy: _____

7. Jerry Maguire, Top Gun, Mission: Impossible: _____

8. Being John Malkovich, There's Something About Mary, Charlie's Angels: _____

9. Lethal Weapon, Braveheart, The Patriot: _____

10. Pirates of the Caribbean, Edward Scissorhands, Alice in Wonderland: _____

11. Good Will Hunting, Invictus, The Talented Mr. Ripley: _____

12. Gladiator, A Beautiful Mind, Body of Lies: _____

13. Batman & Robin, Three Kings, The Perfect Storm: _____

14. Philadelphia, Big, Forrest Gump: _____

15. Speed, The Blind Side, Miss Congeniality: _____

```
H Y N E W O R C L L E S S U R
C E Y H I T V B X H J C J K K
A R E L L I T S N E B H U C B
M R N U L N F I P E N T L O R
E A O Q S G T W P W O R I L M
R C O B M Q Q G E D M C A L V
O M L Y I T X K D V A K R U T
N I C W T O Q Y Y X D R O B O
D J E F H M F J N B T J B A M
I C G Y Q H D M N R T I E R C
A A R F S A J Q H H A C R D R
Z P O J B N F Z O Q M X T N U
K A E C A K J D J F L C S A I
E I G N O S B I G L E M Z S S
Y N A M D I K E L O C I N V E
```

CROSSWORD

ACROSS

1. Pond growth
5. Elegant quality
10. Bolshevik target
14. Catherine ___, last wife of Henry VIII
15. Milk, in Madrid
16. Backscratcher target
17. Genesis brother
18. "High Noon," for one
19. Coin of the Continent
20. Actor who was awarded the Audubon Medal
23. Reznor of Nine Inch Nails
24. Air France flier until 2003
25. MPG part
28. Like "The Twilight Zone"
32. Kind of tower
34. "Miss Saigon" locale
37. Best known role of 20 Across
40. Army truant
42. "___ easy to fall in love..." (Buddy Holly)
43. Fake out, on the ice
44. Actress born in Darjeeling, India
47. Soldier's leave referred to by its initials
48. "The Little Mermaid" mermaid
49. High-tech surgical tool
51. "Life of Pi" director
52. Maple extract
55. Pays month-to-month
59. Best known role of 44 Across
64. Addition, subtraction and such
66. Mother, in Mexico
67. Mine entrance
68. "See ya," in Pisa
69. Tear-jerker in the kitchen
70. Bunyan's Blue Ox
71. "Not ___ eye in the house"
72. Clarinet player's needs
73. Flexible Flyer, e.g.

DOWN

1. Away from each other
2. Repair bill line
3. Loon relative
4. Actress Dahl
5. Thicken, as cream
6. Edward who wrote "The Owl and the Pussycat"
7. Entr'___ (play interlude)
8. Garden buildings
9. Peasants of yore
10. Cake level
11. Five-card or seven-card game
12. Horizontal: Abbr.
13. Letter between pi and sigma
21. They're numbered on maps (Abbr.)
22. Ear-related
26. Christensen of "Parenthood"
27. Actress Winona
29. Archeological site

30. Like many conglomerates: Abbr.
31. Famous Ford flop
33. "Mamaji" author ___ Mehta
34. Having to do with ships
35. Hawn film "Bird on ___"
36. 20- or 44-Across, e.g.
38. China's place
39. Rich yuletide drinks
41. Tell a whopper
45. Feline female of film
46. Dragon slayer
50. Fixes up, as an old house

53. Galahad's garb
54. Hangar occupant
56. Tennis champ Rafael
57. "The ___ has spoken"
    ("Survivor" catchphrase)
58. Filled to the brim
60. Bok ___ (Chinese vegetable)
61. "Nurse Jackie" star Falco
62. Crushed underfoot
63. Hamilton bills
64. Motown owner since 1988
65. Give a hand to

Answers on page 377.

STAR & ROLE

Solve the puzzle using 8 remaining letters. HINT: The real-life inspiration is not nearly as handsome.

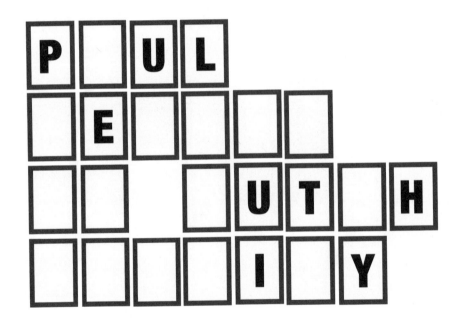

Answers on page 377.

WORD LADDER

Change just one letter on each line to go from the top word to the bottom word. Do not change the order of the letters. You must have a common English word or a name at each step.

DATE

———

———

———

———

FILM

THINGS

Solve the puzzle using 4 remaining letters. HINT: Looking back at the glory days.

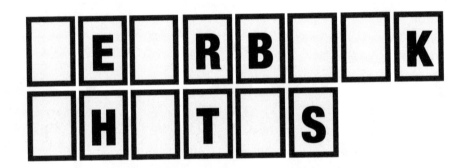

Answers on page 377.

LIVING THINGS

Solve the puzzle using 4 remaining letters. HINT: They have a unique whistle instead of a name.

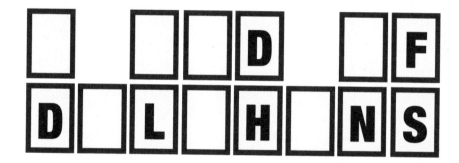

ADDAGRAMs

These two puzzles function exactly like an anagram with an added step: In addition to being scrambled, each set of four words below is missing the same letter. Discover the missing letter, then unscramble the words.

TARGETS

ASPENS

MARTINET

THROW

TRAIL

UNCLES

VERTICAL

MISTRAL

Answers on page 377.

SAME LETTER

Solve the puzzle using 4 remaining letters. HINT: Ironically, most modern-day SUVs don't qualify as this, taxwise.

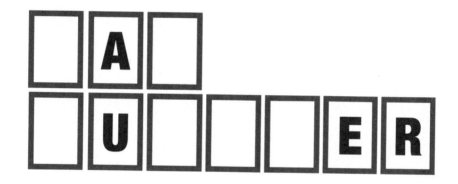

THEY COME IN THREES

Every word listed below is contained within the group of letters. Words can be found in a straight line horizontally, vertically, or diagonally. They may read either forward or backward.

AMIGOS

BASE HIT

CARD MONTE

DEGREES

DOG NIGHT

GRACES

IRON

LEGGED RACE

LITTLE WORDS

PIECE SUIT

POINT TURN

RING CIRCUS

SOME

STOOGES

STRIKES

TIMES A LADY

TOED SLOTH

WHEELER

WISE MEN

WISHES

WOOD

```
      H G H T O L S D E O T
      Z L S D R O W E L T T I L
      B E O P I E C E S U I T M D X
      A M I G O S F Y I T I H E S A B
      E V Y I           R F G S E S S
                        O I A C R V
                        N L A C K
                        Z G A R L
                        W O O D G
            F K F D Y K I D Y
            B D E G R E E S
            S T R I K E S C H
                        F L F R E
                        A E T Q S
                        N E T R R
                        O R O H E O
      S G Z C           M K O Y J W M
      N M Z S E C A R D E G G E L N P
      P O I N T T U R N E M E S I W
      Q F B B U A M S V A D S C
```

CROSSWORD

ACROSS
1. "Memory" musical
5. Cultural stuff
9. Makes an even-steven trade
14. Gal pal, in Paris
15. Wield a whisk
16. Wore
17. Gp. of battalions
18. Block of hay
19. Coral ring
20. Plea that may have a cherry on top
23. Proofreader's find
24. Take away (from)
28. Cobb and Pennington
29. Boosters, for short
33. Kidney-shaped nut
34. Beetle-shaped amulet
36. Supergirl's birth name
37. Vow made with little digits
41. "___ my day!"
42. Beauty-pageant crowns
43. Chill command
46. Family tree member: Abbr.
47. Bill Nye's subj.
50. Salt holders
52. Gets better
54. Records clerk, e.g.
58. Melodies
61. Cool drinks

62. "Two Mules for Sister ___" (Clint Eastwood film)
63. Valuable quality
64. Meal for a carnivore
65. Cleveland's lake
66. Lizard that can climb walls
67. Talk back
68. Formula for salt

DOWN
1. Magical conveyance
2. "...___ old soul"
3. Shere Khan and Tigger
4. Brief fracas
5. Dear columnist
6. Operate a harvester
7. Like Shaquille O'Neal
8. Jouster's horse
9. Kind of daisy
10. Gear for an aquatic sport
11. Fuss and bother
12. Office seeker, informally
13. NBC comedy show since '75
21. Trail closely
22. Bygone nuclear agcy.
25. Cries of insight
26. Coat with wax
27. "Up, up and away" flier, once
30. Month after "Avril"
31. ___-à-porter (ready to wear)
32. Pleasantly flavorful
34. Privileged preview
35. Hillside in Scotland
37. Garden walk

38. Build-it-yourself furniture company
39. Surg. theaters
40. ___ Picchu (site of Incan ruins)
41. Barker and Kettle, e.g.
44. Takes care of
45. Marine eagle
47. Largest desert
48. Man of the cloth
49. Netanyahu's nation

51. Con jobs
53. German steel town
55. Cartoon light bulb
56. Grassy fields
57. Attention-getting sounds
58. Dog's ID
59. "___ as directed"
60. President's foreign policy grp.

PHRASE

Solve the puzzle using 7 remaining letters. HINT: Your wallet is safe as long as you don't press purchase.

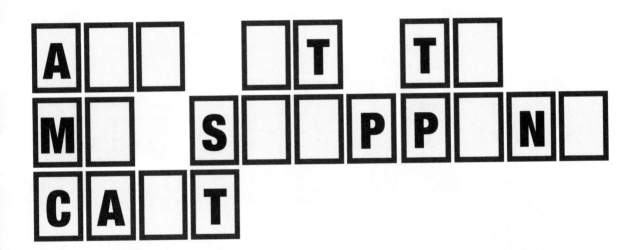

Answers on page 377.

THINGS

Solve the puzzle using 8 remaining letters. HINT: Don't go chasing...

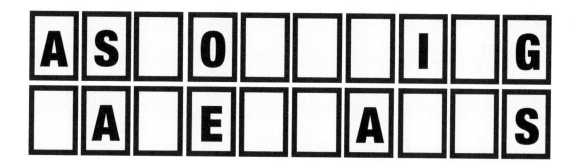

SHIRLEY TEMPLE

We're sure you can run ring(lets) around this puzzle! Words can be found in a straight line horizontally, vertically, or diagonally, and may read forward or backward. Leftover letters reveal a piece of trivia about this screen legend.

AMBASSADOR
"ANIMAL CRACKERS IN MY SOUP"
BABY TAKE A BOW
BRIGHT EYES
CHILD STAR
CURLY TOP
DIMPLES
DIPLOMAT
FORT APACHE
"GOODNIGHT MY LOVE"
HONEYMOON
I'LL BE SEEING YOU
JUST AROUND THE CORNER

KATHLEEN
KISS AND TELL
THE LITTLE COLONEL
THE LITTLE PRINCESS
THE LITTLEST REBEL
MISS ANNIE ROONEY
NOW AND FOREVER
"ON THE GOOD SHIP LOLLIPOP"
POOR LITTLE RICH GIRL
SINCE YOU WENT AWAY
STAND UP AND CHEER
STOWAWAY
WEE WILLIE WINKIE

Trivia:

```
A S H E J E I E V O L Y M T H G I N D O O G
N N S P U K I S S A N D T E L L I R E D P H
E R I S S O A K R E V E R O F D N A W O N W
N T C M T I O T N C K T C A I L T H P E S H
I H L R A O L L H I E Y T U E M P I L E S L
I E E S R L W L A L W N O N R A L L C E O R
H L B O O L C A B I E E C S D L R I Y N K I
M I E A U D H R W E E E I E O W Y E I T H G
G T R I N N I G A A S E N L R A T T L E O H
R T T L D E L M O C Y E P P L H N L O I M C
E L S S T O D D A G K I E M G I R E N P R I
A E E D H I S N E A H E N I D O W R A N O R
G P L E E J T U I S C E R D N A N E D I D E
S R T G C A A R D N I B S S H G E D E W A L
I I T T O H R O T A M O L P I D Y A M W S T
A N I R R A O H O N E Y M O O N S O C H S T
I C L N N G F O R T A P A C H E M O U C A I
H E E E E R R Y A W O B A E K A T Y B A B L
N S H H R D Y E N O O R E I N N A S S I M R
L S T H E L I T T L E C O L O N E L E O A O
M N S I N C E Y O U W E N T A W A Y O N U O
O S L I R E E H C D N A P U D N A T S C E P
```

SPIRAL: CLASSIC MOVIES

Spirals offer a novel twist on the crossword puzzle. Instead of words intersecting, they overlap. The last letters of one word form the first letters of the next word. Words bend around corners as necessary—always heading inward toward the center of the spiral.

1. Greta _____

2. Humphrey _____

3. Actor, musician, or painter

4. _____ Laurel

5. "The Blue _____"
(Marlene Dietrich movie)

6. _____ Burstyn

7. Bring enjoyment to audiences

8. Cowboy's traditional foe

9. _____ Bancroft

10. Patricia _____

11. Alan _____

12. _____ O. Selznick

13. _____ Lupino

4. Blythe _____

15. _____ Borgnine

16. _____ Parsons

17. Jack _____

18. Yves _____

19. _____ Warhol

20. _____ Cannon

21. _____ Lansbury

22. _____ Turner

23. 1968 Luis Buñuel film

24. _____ Starr

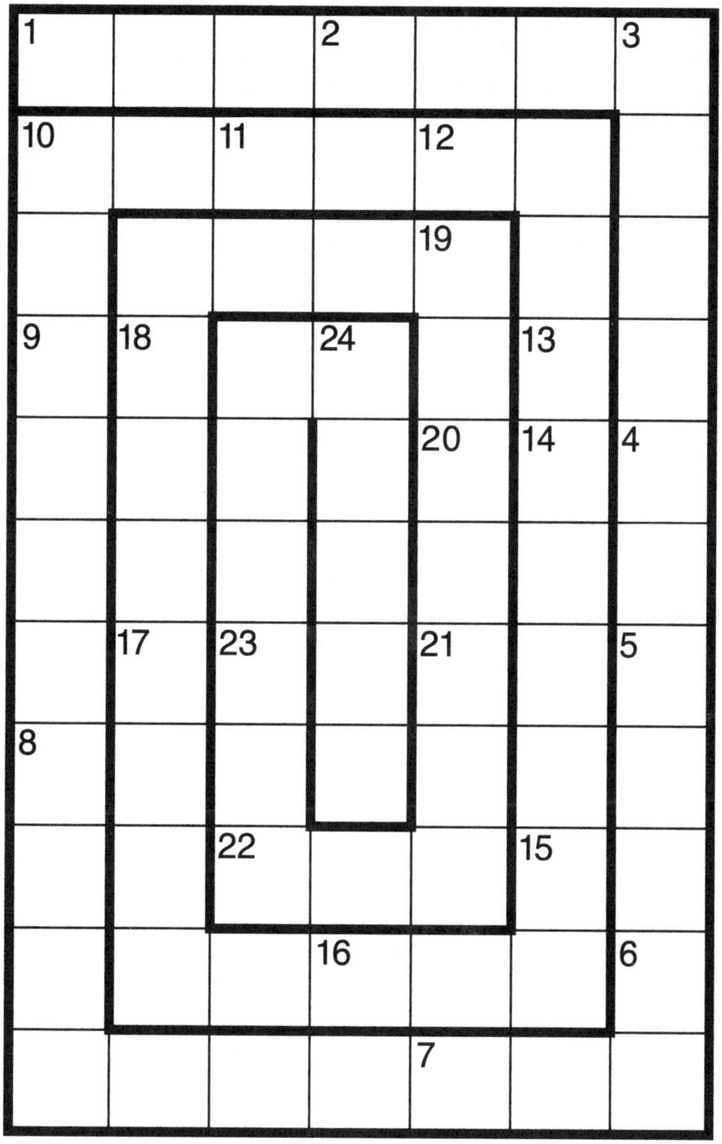
1
2
3
10
11
12
19
9
18
24
13
20
14
4
17
23
21
5
8
22
15
16
6
7

Answers on page 378.

STAR & ROLE

Solve the puzzle using 6 remaining letters. HINT: With two Emmy Awards for the role, she really must be *good*.

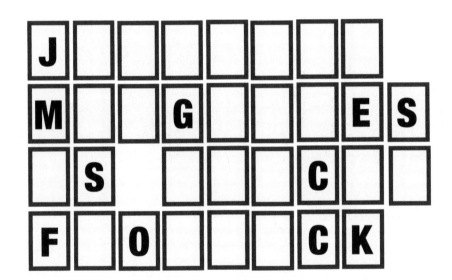

Answers on page 378.

SAME LETTER

Solve the puzzle using 7 remaining letters. HINT: To step on one in bare feet is a rite of passage.

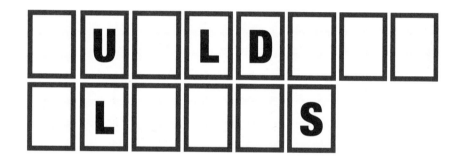

Answers on page 378.

MYTHOLOGY

The letters in the name MARS can be found in boxes 3, 4, 6, and 23, but not necessarily in that order. The same is true for the other mythological names listed below. Using the names and the box numbers as your guide, insert all the letters of the alphabet into the boxes. If you do this correctly, the shaded cells will reveal 2 more names.

Hint: Look for words that share a single letter.

ACHILLES: 1, 2, 4, 6, 9, 15, 20
AJAX: 4, 10, 19
APHRODITE: 1, 2, 3, 4, 5, 13, 15, 17, 24
APOLLO: 4, 9, 13, 24
BACCHUS: 1, 4, 6, 11, 18, 20
FLORA: 3, 4, 8, 9, 13
GORGONS: 3, 6, 12, 13, 14
HYDRA: 1, 3, 4, 5, 22
JUPITER: 2, 3, 10, 11, 15, 17, 24
MARS: 3, 4, 6, 23
NIKE: 2, 12, 15, 21
VENUS: 2, 6, 11, 12, 16
ZEUS: 2, 6, 7, 11

1	2	3	4	5	6	7	8	9	10	11	12	13

14	15	16	17	18	19	20	21	22	23	24	25	26

Answers on page 378.

OPPOSITES

Use the letters below to fill in the boxes and reveal the 2 related words. Connected boxes share the same letter.

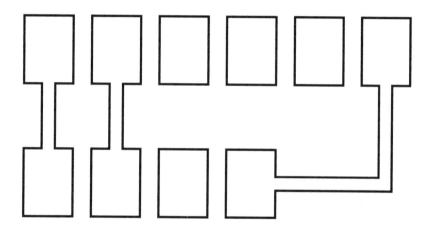

CEIRTUV

SAME LETTER

Solve the puzzle using 6 remaining letters. HINT: Freeze your credit card afterward.

Answers on page 379.

SAME LETTER

Solve the puzzle using 4 remaining letters. HINT:
Considered a favorite Chipotle order.

W-TO-W

This puzzle follows the rules of your typical word search: Every word listed is contained within the group of letters. Words can be found in a straight line horizontally, vertically, or diagonally. They may read either forward or backward. But, in this version, words wrap up, down, and around the 3 sides of the cube.

WALLOW

WARSAW

WAR WIDOW

WEEPING WILLOW

WHEELBARROW

WHEW

WHIPSAW

WHITLOW

WILD WEST SHOW

WILLIWAW

WINDOW

WINDROW

WINSLOW

WITCHES' BREW

WITHDRAW

WITHDREW

WOODROW

WOOD SCREW

WORK CREW

WORKFLOW

WORLDVIEW

SPLIT DECISIONS

Fill in each set of empty cells with letters that will create English words reading both across and down. Letters may repeat within a single set. We've completed one set to get you started.

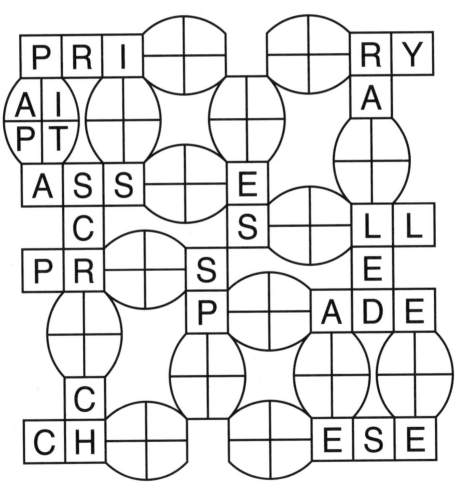

Answers on page 379.

ADDAGRAM

These two puzzles function exactly like an anagram with an added step: In addition to being scrambled, each set of words below is missing the same letter. Discover the missing letter, then unscramble the words.

ANLACE

CICELY

ANKLET

FICHUS

TANDEM

OPPOSE

RULERS

Answers on page 379.

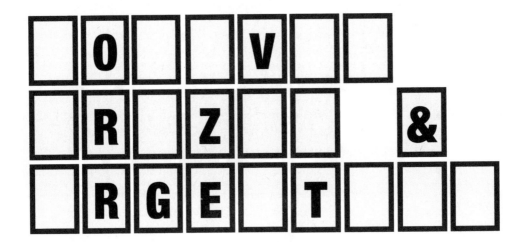

ON THE MAP

Solve the puzzle using 5 remaining letters. HINT: Travel south for warm weather.

	O		V		
	R	Z			&
	R	G	E	T			

ON THE MAP

Solve the puzzle using 6 remaining letters. HINT: If you live in Seattle, this is the perfect weekend escape.

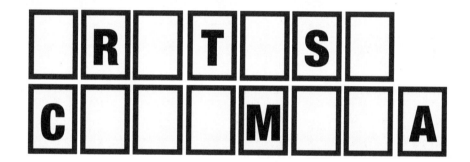

```
[ ] R [ ] T [ ] S [ ]
C [ ] [ ] [ ] M [ ] A
```

LETTERBOX BIG SCREEN

The letters in Marx can be found in boxes 1, 2, 11, and 20, but not necessarily in that order. The same is true for the other actors' names listed below. Using the names and the box numbers that follow them to guide you, insert all the letters of the alphabet into the boxes. If you do this correctly, the shaded cells will reveal 2 more film stars.

BULLOCK: 6, 7, 15, 19, 21, 26

CLIFT: 7, 8, 13, 16, 19

DE NIRO: 3, 6, 8, 9, 20, 24

GIBSON: 3, 4, 6, 8, 15, 18

JACKSON: 3, 4, 5, 6, 11, 19, 26

KIDMAN: 1, 3, 8, 11, 24, 26

MARX: 1, 2, 11, 20

McQUEEN: 1, 3, 9, 19, 21, 25

PACINO: 3, 6, 8, 11, 17, 19

SCHWARZENEGGER: 3, 4, 9, 11, 12, 18, 19, 20, 22, 23

SMITH: 1, 4, 8, 16, 23

VALENTINO: 3, 6, 7, 8, 9, 10, 11, 16

WAYNE: 3, 9, 11, 12, 14

1	2	3	4	5	6	7	8	9	10	11	12	13

14	15	16	17	18	19	20	21	22	23	24	25	26

Answers on page 379.

SAME LETTER

Solve the puzzle using 5 remaining letters. HINT: Trouble doesn't stir itself up.

PROPER NAME

Solve the puzzle using 4 remaining letters. HINT:
Famously danced in *Magic Mike*.

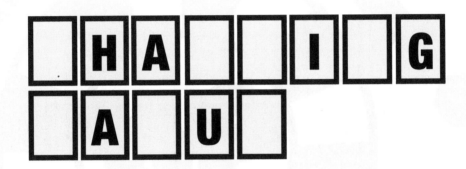

Answers on page 379.

THING

Solve the puzzle using 6 remaining letters. HINT: Studying hard pays off.

ON THE MAP

Solve the puzzle using 6 remaining letters. HINT: This mountain nation is known for its measure of gross national happiness.

Answers on page 379.

DIAMOND CUT

Follow the arrows to solve each clue and complete the grid.

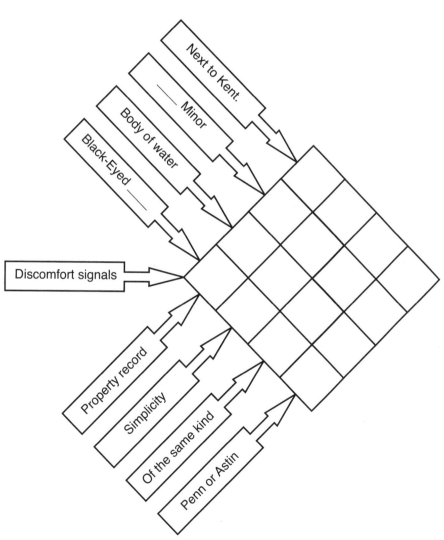

- Next to Kent.
- _____ Minor
- Body of water
- Black-Eyed _____
- Discomfort signals
- Property record
- Simplicity
- Of the same kind
- Penn or Astin

ITALY

Every word listed below is contained within the group of letters. Words can be found in a straight line horizontally, vertically, or diagonally. They may read either forward or backward. The leftover letters spell out an additional fact.

ANTIPASTO	PARMESAN
ARMANI	PASTA
COLOSSEUM	PISA
DANTE	PIZZA
ESPRESSO	POPE
FIAT	RISOTTO
FLORENCE	ROME
GENOA	SICILY
MACHIAVELLI	TINTORETTO
MICHELANGELO	TUSCANY
MILAN	VENICE
NAPLES	VERDI

```
            N M P I
          T A L U A A I Y I E
      S   O N E S S L F Z T
  Y L I C I S T I E O I N Z
  F T O T S A P I T N A M H A
  E F L O R E N C E D T
G I L L E V A I H C A M
R O T T E R O T N I T
C E A     T I L C A D
  E     N S E T S R E
        R O G I E E S
        G O T N N M V
        E F T A A R
        N A O L M A
          O S S E R P S E E
          A R N H A T P
              A C O R Y A
              N P I O N D F A
              L M A   S H
              E C
              C S I
              I U O
              N T
              E N
              V
```

SAME LETTER

Solve the puzzle using 4 remaining letters. HINT: You better hide these from Bugs Bunny.

Answers on page 380.

AROUND THE HOUSE

Solve the puzzle using 4 remaining letters. HINT: Many Barbie girls.

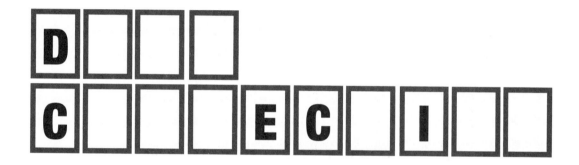

Answers on page 380.

CODE-DOKU

Solve this puzzle just as you would a sudoku. Use deductive logic to complete the grid so that each row, column, and 3 by 3 box contains the letters from the word LONGITUDE.

U				N				
N		T	I				L	
		L					G	
		I	N					
	O	G		D		L	E	
				G	O			
	I					T		
	U				O	G		D
			I					U

Answers on page 380.

ADDAGRAM

These two puzzles function exactly like an anagram with an added step: In addition to being scrambled, each set of words below is missing the same letter. Discover the missing letter, then unscramble the words.

RABBLE

BICKER

NECTAR

CONFERS

HEFT

AXE MEN

STATE

GIVEN

Answers on page 380.

LIVING THINGS

Solve the puzzle using 5 remaining letters. HINT: Quack,
Quack! Honk, Honk!

Answers on page 380.

AROUND THE HOUSE

Solve the puzzle using 7 remaining letters. HINT: Keeps your skin smooth and shiny.

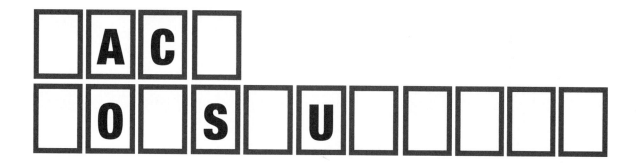

SAME LETTER

Solve the puzzle using 4 remaining letters. HINT: Sealed with a kiss.

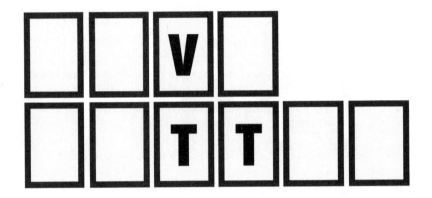

Answers on page 380.

ON THE MAP

Solve the puzzle using 6 remaining letters. HINT: Its residents share a nickname with a fuzzy flightless bird.

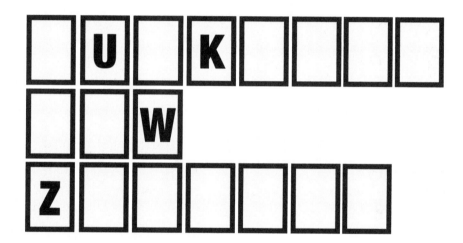

THING

Solve the puzzle using 5 remaining letters. HINT:
Everyone has a different recipe.

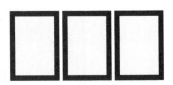

Answers on page 380.

WHAT ARE YOU DOING?

Solve the puzzle using 6 remaining letters. HINT: It's important not just to donate but to volunteer as well.

Answers on page 380.

BEFORE & AFTER

Solve the puzzle using 5 remaining letters. HINT: Served with a bagel?

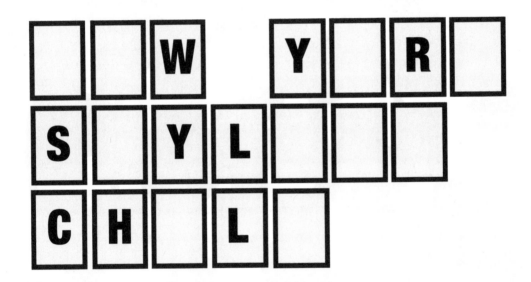

ELEVATOR WORDS

Like an elevator, words move up and down the "floors" of this puzzle. Starting with the first answer, the second part of each answer carries down to become the first part of the following answer. With the clues given, complete the puzzle.

1. Purse _____   1. Financial resources

2. _____ _____   2. Conditional

3. _____ _____   3. It's much appreciated on those stormy winter days

4. _____ _____   4. Clearance of a sort

5. _____ _____   5. Mall advertisement

6. _____-_____   6. Competitive technique

7. _____ board   7. Kitchen device

Answers on page 381.

ELEVATOR WORDS

Like an elevator, words move up and down the "floors" of this puzzle. Starting with the first answer, the second part of each answer carries down to become the first part of the following answer. With the clues given, complete the puzzle.

1. Laughing _____   1. Dentist's helper

2. _____ _____   2. Fuel pipeline

3. _____   3. The Lower 48, to a Hawaiian

4. _____ _____   4. Sailor's cry

5. _____-_____   5. Indifferent

6. _____   6. Bah follower

7. _____-eyed   7. Agog

Answers on page 381.

BEFORE & AFTER

Solve the puzzle using 6 remaining letters. HINT: They especially like group projects.

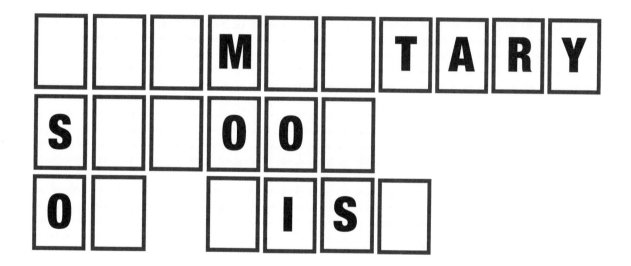

LANDMARK

Solve the puzzle using 3 remaining letters. HINT: Nashville's most famous stage.

Answers on page 381.

RHYME TIME

Solve the puzzle using 5 remaining letters. HINT: The answer to a man's greatest mystery.

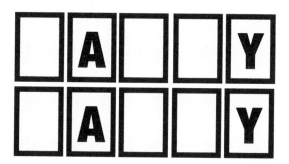

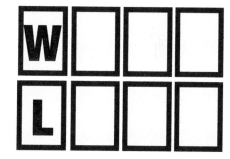

SQUARE WORDS

This puzzle follows the rules of your typical word search: Every word listed is contained within the group of letters. Words can be found in a straight line horizontally, vertically, or diagonally. They may read either forward or backward. But, in this version, words wrap up, down, and around the 3 sides of the cube.

ACRE

BERKELEY

CARPENTER'S

DANCE

DEAL

FEET

FOLEY

FOUR

HAYMARKET

HERALD

INCH

KNOT

LAFAYETTE

LATIN

LEICESTER

MAGIC

MEAL

MEASURE

METER

MILE

NUMBER

PERFECT

RIGGER

ROOT

SHOOTER

ST. JAMES'S

TIMES

TOWN

TRAFALGAR

UNION

WASHINGTON

WORD

YARD

313

BEFORE & AFTER

Solve the puzzle using 5 remaining letters. HINT: A rare creature come Mother's Day.

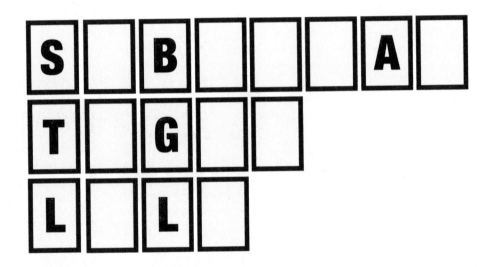

Answers on page 381.

ELEVATOR WORDS

Like an elevator, words move up and down the "floors" of this puzzle. Starting with the first answer, the second part of each answer carries down to become the first part of the following answer. With the clues given, complete the puzzle.

1. Kettle _____

2. _____ _____

3. _____ _____

4. _____ _____

5. _____ _____

6. _____ _____

7. _____ bench

1. Small percussion instrument

2. Marching band leader

3. Member of the top brass with two stars

4. A place to find almost anything you need

5. He's often after shoplifters

6. Police investigation

7. Table for a carpenter

Answers on page 381.

THING

Solve the puzzle using 5 remaining letters. HINT: Can stick with you long after you graduate.

SHOW BIZ

Solve the puzzle using 5 remaining letters. HINT: Bradley Cooper became a triple threat entertainer when he adapted *A Star Is Born*.

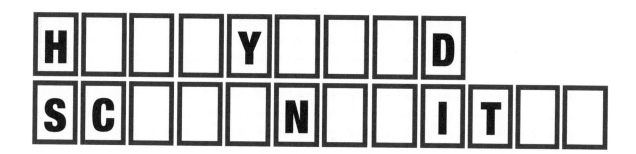

H			Y			D		
S	C				N		I	T		

Answers on page 381.

BEFORE & AFTER

1. Find a word that completes the first word or phrase and begins the second. For example, the answer to Clue #1 is "butterfly." The number of blanks tells you the number of letters in each missing middle word. (Hint: The missing words are in alphabetical order.)

2. As you go, circle the missing words in the butterfly-shaped grid on page 15. Words can be found horizontally, vertically, or diagonally. If you can't figure out a missing word from the clues, look for words in the grid, which will help you solve the fill-in-the-blank.

3. Once you've circled all the words in the grid, the leftover letters will spell an observation about certain commercials you see on TV.

CLUES

1. MONARCH _ _ _ _ _ _ _ _ _ KISS
2. HAPPY AS A _ _ _ _ CHOWDER
3. LINCOLN _ _ _ _ _ _ _ _ _ _ _ DRIFT
4. TENNIS _ _ _ _ _ JESTER
5. WAY OFF IN THE _ _ _ _ _ _ _ _ RUNNER
6. LONG _ _ _ _ _ _ _ _ _ OF LABOR
7. BODY _ _ _ _ _ _ JEOPARDY
8. ROMAN _ _ _ _ _ _ _ PENGUIN
9. THE KING'S _ _ _ _ _ _ _ _ MUFFIN
10. GO _ _ _ _ _ _ OF SPEECH
11. FENCING _ _ _ _ _ _ OF CEREMONIES
12. U.S. _ _ _ _ _ SESAME

318

13. GOLDEN _ _ _ _ _ _ _ _ _ _ _ KNOCKS
14. SURPRISE _ _ _ _ _ POOPER
15. PICTURE _ _ _ _ _ _ _ PITCH
16. STRIP _ _ _ _ _ FACE
17. THAT'S A GOOD _ _ _ _ _ _ _ _ MARK
18. DOWNWARD _ _ _ _ _ _ NOTEBOOK
19. ACORN _ _ _ _ _ _ RACQUET
20. BUMPER _ _ _ _ _ _ _ SHOCK
21. NYLON _ _ _ _ _ _ _ _ _ STUFFER
22. I.Q. _ _ _ _ TUBE
23. DOUBTING _ _ _ _ _ _ AQUINAS
24. DENZEL _ _ _ _ _ _ _ _ _ _ POST

Leftover letters:

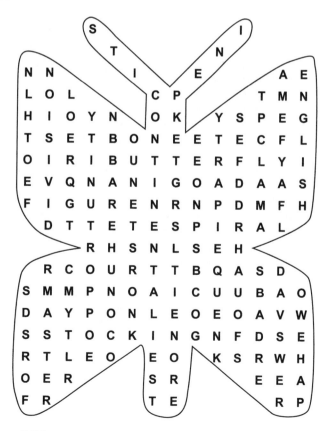

Answers on page 381.

SHOW BIZ

Solve the puzzle using 7 remaining letters. HINT: At 007 the sky will fall.

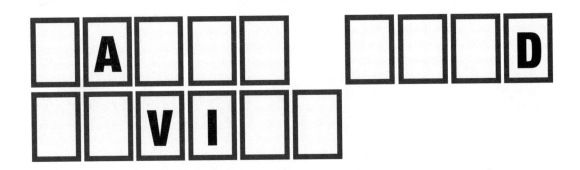

Answers on page 381.

WHAT ARE YOU WEARING?

Solve the puzzle using 5 remaining letters. HINT: Why buy clothing when you can make your own?

CROSSWORD

ACROSS

1. Church offshoot
5. Creepy lab guy
9. Noncom nickname
14. "So funny!"
15. It comes and goes
16. Rap sheet handle
17. What bar patrons may run
18. Casino machine
19. Auto dealer's offer
20. JOY TO THE ... ? [venerable reference work]
23. Racing sledders
24. Hoosier State (Abbr.)
25. Punk rocker Vicious
28. Abbr. in many Québec addresses
29. Available for ready reference
32. Spray cops carry
33. Grant-___ (government funding)
34. "Eight Is Enough" actor Willie
35. IN THE PRIME OF ... ? [flotation device]
39. Feudal laborers
40. Neck backs
41. "Pardon me," British style
42. "Get started!"
44. Dad's other half
47. Letter add-ons, for short
48. Downing Street number

49. Car trim
51. FROM TOP TO ... ? [catfish, e.g.]
54. Ballet slipper fabric
57. Hip bones
58. Stockbroker's advice, at times
59. Colorful marble
60. African country where Timbuktu is
61. Buttery spread
62. Carryall bags
63. Cycle stuntman Knievel
64. Electrical power unit

DOWN

1. Shoulder wraps
2. Dine at a diner
3. Card it
4. Agree to discuss later
5. "Piece of cake!"
6. Fish feature
7. Lamar of the NBA
8. Regular price
9. Tossed dish
10. One of the Baldwin brothers
11. Spanish estuary
12. Fuel for a Ford
13. 180° from WNW
21. Pilotless planes
22. Opposite from SSW
25. Bar reorder, with "the"
26. Cake decorator
27. ___ Moines, IA
30. Balsam source
31. Dog tag, for short
32. Mark Cuban's team, for short

33. Far from certain
34. "We ___ World"
35. In proverbs it's more
36. 401(k) alternatives
37. Brazil's ___ Paulo
38. Not just a mess-up, in modern lingo
39. Draw on a straw
42. Eagles hit "___ Over It"
43. How trains run, ideally
44. Ford introduced in 1928

45. Dish you might flip over?
46. Red-wine grape
48. Phone button sounds
50. Plant seeds again
51. Take the lure
52. A king of Norway
53. Roger Bannister's race
54. Formed a lap
55. Long, long follower
56. Body art, for short

Answers on page 382.

PHRASE

Solve the puzzle using 6 remaining letters. HINT: Don't know? Webster probably does.

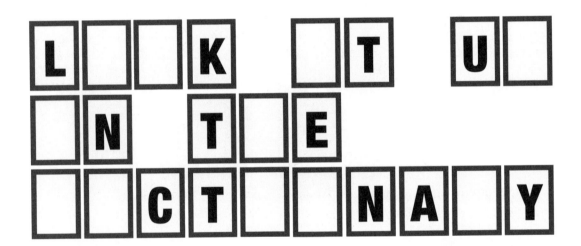

L _ _ K _ T U _
_ N T E _ E
_ _ C T _ _ N A _ Y

Answers on page 382.

THING

Solve the puzzle using 6 remaining letters. HINT: Prominent pieces include *The Starry Night*, *The Kiss*, and *The Scream*.

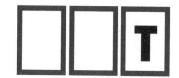

FAMOUS "ANDS"

Every word listed below is contained within the group of letters. Words can be found in a straight line horizontally, vertically, or diagonally. They may read either forward or backward.

(BONNIE &) CLYDE

(ABBOTT &) COSTELLO

(BLACK &) DECKER

(MAYNARD &) DOBIE

(PROCTOR &) GAMBLE

(LAUREL &) HARDY

(OZZIE &) HARRIET

(STARSKY &) HUTCH

(PEANUT BUTTER &) JELLY

(BEN &) JERRY

(JOHNSON &)JOHNSON

(BATMAN &) ROBIN

(LAVERNE &) SHIRLEY

(WILLIE &) WAYLON

(SMITH &) WESSON

```
M P E M Q E Y H N Y W
R G T I D M K A Y M X
W M A Y B J N R E R J
O E L M E O K R L E O
L C S R B H D I R K H
L R R S U L K E I C N
E Y F T O Y E T H E S
T Q C V L N D T S D O
S H K L N O L Y A W N
O R E N H A R D Y G K
C J Y D Q L R O B I N
```

OCCUPATION

Solve the puzzle using 5 remaining letters. HINT: Directs musical performances.

```
[ ][ ][ ][H][S][T][ ][A]
[ ][ ][N][U][T][ ][ ]
```

Answers on page 382.

PHRASE

Solve the puzzle using 6 remaining letters. HINT: Generosity keeps moving.

ELEVATOR WORDS

Like an elevator, words move up and down the "floors" of this puzzle. Starting with the first answer, the second part of each answer carries down to become the first part of the following answer. With the clues given, complete the puzzle.

1. Curtain _____

2. _____ _____

3. _____

4. _____ _____

5. _____ _____

6. _____ _____

7. _____ run

1. Appearance at the end of a show

2. Where a driver may seek assistance

3. Train unit

4. In England, place to keep your wheels

5. Outdoor resting spot

6. Case without a jury

7. Test of a sort

Answers on page 382.

BEFORE & AFTER

Solve the puzzle using 4 remaining letters. HINT: Flying is a royal pain.

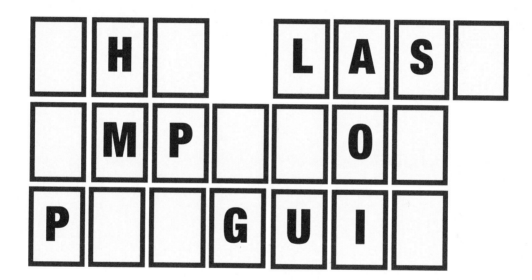

FOOD & DRINK

Solve the puzzle using 5 remaining letters. HINT: Which do you prefer, Starbucks or Dunkin'?

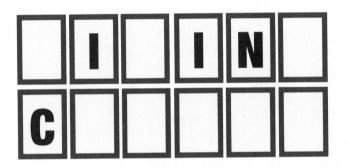

LIVING THINGS

Solve the puzzle using 7 remaining letters. HINT: The opposite of barking dogs.

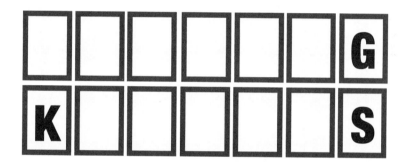

FOOD & DRINK

Solve the puzzle using 5 remaining letters. HINT: The most common fruit found on a pizza.

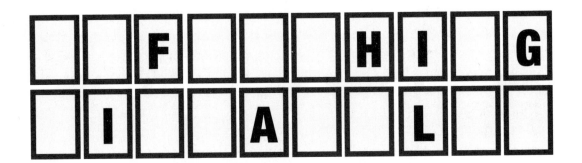

Answers on page 382.

RHYME TIME

Solve the puzzle using 4 remaining letters. HINT: Calm and immaculate.

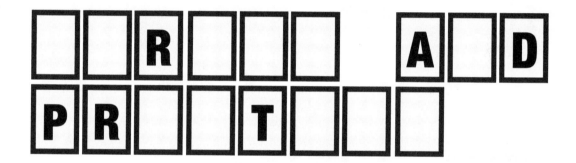

WORD

Every word listed below is contained within the group of letters. Words can be found in a straight line horizontally, vertically, or diagonally. They may read either forward or backward.

AFTER

BUZZ

CATCH

CROSS

ENCOURAGING

EQUIVALENT

FORE

FOUR-LETTER

GOOD

LAST

MONOSYLLABIC

PASS

POLYSYLLABIC

PORTMANTEAU

ROOT

SPOKEN

SWEAR

WATCH

WRITTEN

```
B T N E L A V I U Q E S W
M O R E T T E L R U O F S
P O L Y S Y L L A B I C E
O R N A K N O D E X U N M
R S P O K E N U W G C Z Q
T S A L S R L P S O I U Z
M E S Y N Y O E U O W H A
A G S F E T L R W D C S Y
N F O U T A A L I T K S V
T R T G T G D U A H L S W
E J X E I W P C U B Q O F
A O B N R N F U T W I R Z
U N G N W A T C H H J C K
```

Answers on page 382.

FUN & GAMES

Solve the puzzle using 6 remaining letters. HINT: Shaun White is a three-time Olympic gold medalist.

				B	A		D	I		

Answers on page 382.

FOOD & DRINK

Solve the puzzle using 6 remaining letters. HINT: Sour cream, cream cheese, mayonnaise, parmesan, and a touch of green leaves.

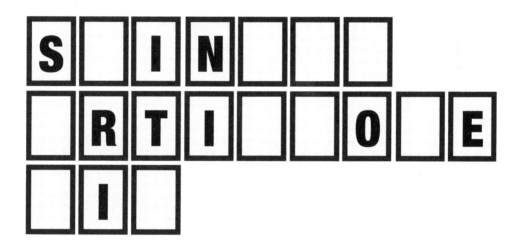

339

Answers on page 382.

BEFORE & AFTER

Solve the puzzle using 5 remaining letters. HINT: Rates go up, up, and away!

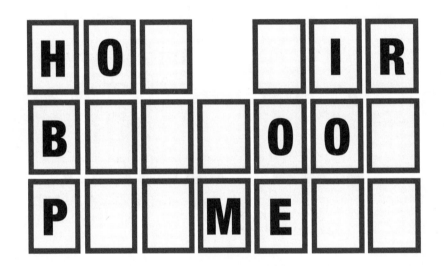

Answers on page 383.

ELEVATOR WORDS

Like an elevator, words move up and down the "floors" of this puzzle. Starting with the first answer, the second part of each answer carries down to become the first part of the following answer. With the clues given, complete the puzzle.

1. Lemon _____

2. _____ _____

3. _____ _____

4. _____ _____

5. _____ _____

6. _____ _____

7. _____ sense

1. Brownie alternative

2. Scanning products at the checkout counter

3. Emergency situation

4. Songbird

5. Sound-check instruction

6. Mr. Ed, e.g.

7. Savvy

Answers on page 383.

FIT IT

4 LETTERS

CALI

GIZA

KIEV

LIMA

ROMA

5 LETTERS

BOGOR

CAIRO

DELHI

DHAKA

OSAKA

PARIS

PUSAN

TOKYO

6 LETTERS

ANKARA

BOGOTA

BOMBAY

INCHON

LAHORE

LONDON

MADRID

MALANG

MOSCOW

SYDNEY

TAIPEI

TEHRAN

7 LETTERS

BAGHDAD

BANGKOK

CHICAGO

JAKARTA

KARACHI

NEW YORK

TORONTO

8 LETTERS

BRASILIA

BUDAPEST

HONG KONG

ISTANBUL

KINSHASA

SANTIAGO

SAO PAULO

SHANGHAI

YOKOHAMA

9 LETTERS

BANGALORE

SINGAPORE

10 LETTERS

ADDIS ABABA

ALEXANDRIA

CASABLANCA

LOS ANGELES

MEXICO CITY

11 LETTERS

BUENOS AIRES

12 LETTERS

RIO DE JANEIRO

ST. PETERSBURG

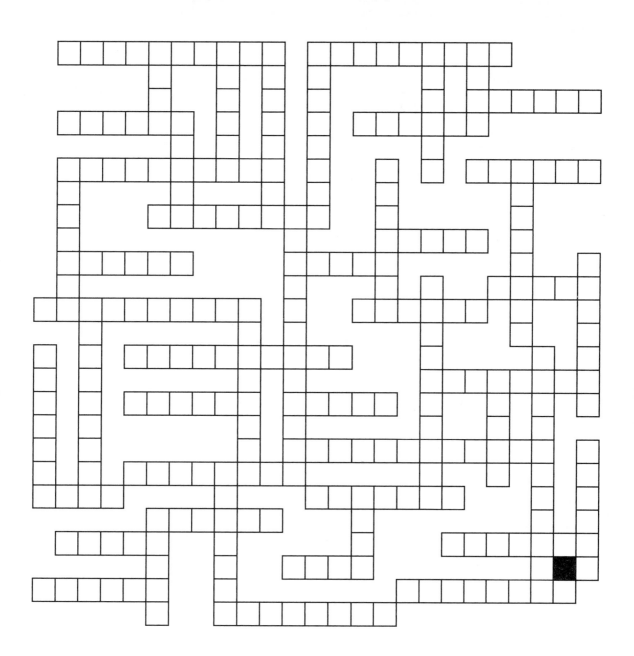

URBAN SPRAWL_p.eps

Answers on page 383.

ON THE MAP

Solve the puzzle using 7 remaining letters. HINT: A Scandinavian capital.

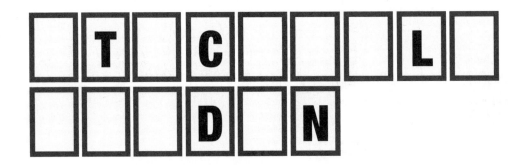

Answers on page 383.

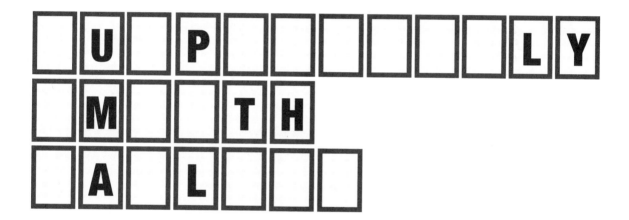

SAME LETTER

Solve the puzzle using 6 remaining letters. HINT: Calm waters on the horizon.

Row 1: ☐ U ☐ P ☐ ☐ ☐ ☐ ☐ ☐ L Y
Row 2: ☐ M ☐ ☐ T H
Row 3: ☐ A ☐ L ☐ ☐

ISLANDS

Complete the word search below to reveal a hidden word related to the puzzle's topic. Every word listed below is contained within the group of letters. Words can be found in a straight line horizontally, vertically, or diagonally. They may read either forward or backward. Once you find all the words, you can read the hidden message from the remaining letters, top to bottom, left to right.

ALAND	MALTA
ALCATRAZ	MAN
BALI	OKI
CORSICA	ORKNEY
CRETE	SAMOA
GALAPAGOS	SARDINIA
HAINAN	SICILY
HONG KONG	SKYE
LONG	TAIWAN
LUZON	YAP

Hidden word:

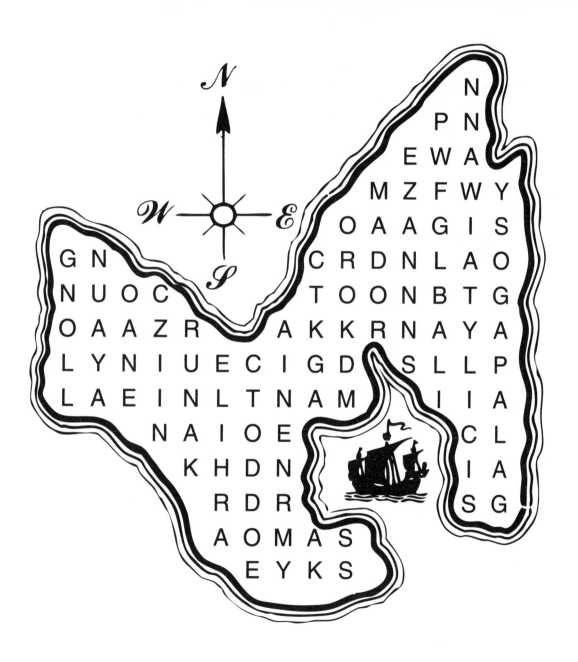

ON THE MAP

Solve the puzzle using 4 remaining letters. HINT: The North Pole is located here.

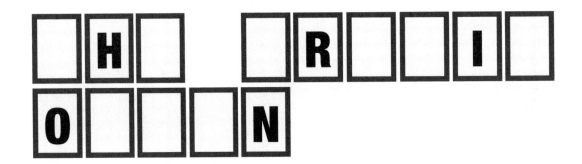

Answers on page 383.

ON THE MAP

Solve the puzzle using 6 remaining letters. HINT: Where you can travel to Paris, Cairo, and NYC all in one day.

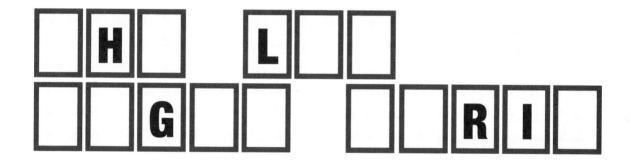

_ H _ _ _ L _ _
_ _ G _ _ _ _ R I _

ROAD WORK

This puzzle follows the rules of your typical word search: Every word listed is contained within the group of letters. Words can be found in a straight line horizontally, vertically, or diagonally. They may read either forward or backward. But, in this version, words wrap up, down, and around the 3 sides of the cube.

ALLEY	DRIVE
AVENUE	HIGHWAY
BOULEVARD	INTERSTATE
BRIDGE	LANE
BYPASS	MEWS
BYWAY	PARKWAY
CIRCLE	ROAD
CLOVERLEAF	STREET
COURT	TERRACE
CRESCENT	THOROUGHFARE
CUL-DE-SAC	THRUWAY
DEAD END	TUNNEL
DETOUR	TURNPIKE

CHARACTER

Solve the puzzle using 5 remaining letters. HINT: Asgardian of the Galaxy.

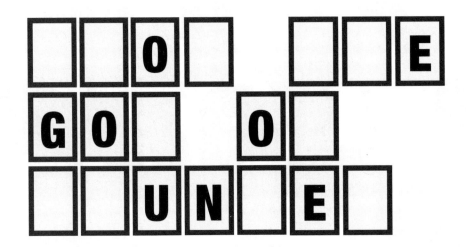

352

Answers on page 384.

THING

Solve the puzzle using 6 remaining letters. HINT: Give a quarter to thank someone for being them.

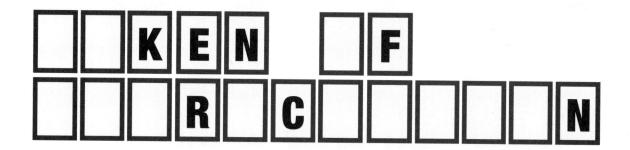

Answers on page 384.

THING

Solve the puzzle using 5 remaining letters. HINT: A stiff rivalry.

Answers on page 384.

FUN & GAMES

Solve the puzzle using 5 remaining letters. HINT: The only object that comes flying back to you.

T				W	I		G	
B			ME				G	

Answers on page 384.

AROUND THE HOUSE

Solve the puzzle using 5 remaining letters. HINT: How to prevent cavities.

Answers on page 384.

WHAT ARE YOU WEARING?

Solve the puzzle using 4 remaining letters. HINT: When winter comes, cover your thumbs.

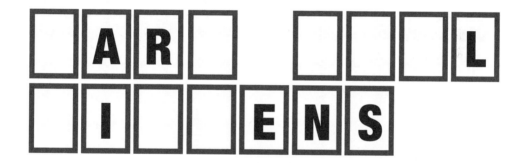

□ A R □   □ □ □ L
□ I □ □ E N S

PHRASE

Solve the puzzle using 6 remaining letters. HINT: It performed wonders.

ANSWER KEY

PAGE 4
WINNIE THE POOH

PAGE 5
YOUNG HONEYMOONERS

PAGE 6
A PRIDE OF LIONS

PAGE 7
CURIOUS RACCOON

PAGE 8
DOROTHY & TOTO

PAGE 9
ELECTRIC RAZOR

PAGE 10
RED ROVER

PAGE 11

M	G	T	I	N	S	Y	C	A
S	N	C	Y	T	A	M	I	G
I	A	Y	G	M	C	S	T	N
T	M	A	N	Y	G	I	S	C
N	Y	S	T	C	I	G	A	M
C	I	G	S	A	M	T	N	Y
Y	S	N	A	G	T	C	M	I
G	T	M	C	I	N	A	Y	S
A	C	I	M	S	Y	N	G	T

PAGE 12
ALUMINUM FOIL

PAGE 13
AVOCADO TOAST

PAGE 14
BEN STILLER

PAGE 15
BOSTON TERRIER

PAGE 16
COTTON SWEATPANTS

PAGE 17
COMPOSER HANS ZIMMER

PAGE 18
A FEAST FIT FOR A KING

PAGE 19
ABRACADABRA

PAGE 20
BROADWAY ACTOR

PAGE 21
CIVIL ENGINEER

PAGE 22
1. MARK; 2. BILL; 3. JACK; 4. CHUCK; 5. ART; 6. WILL

PAGE 23
NEIL DEGRASSE TYSON

ANSWER KEY

PAGES 24-25

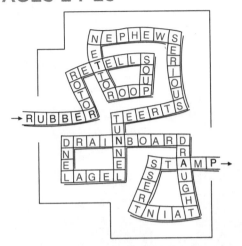

PAGES 26-27

PAGE 28
CAPTURE THE FLAG

PAGE 29
1. GLOVE; 2. FIELD; 3. BASE; 4. BAT;
5. BALL; 6. TEAM

PAGE 30
WOODEN ROLLER COASTER

PAGE 31

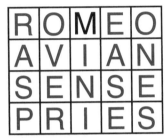

PAGE 32
FEDERAL HOLIDAY

PAGE 33
FRATERNITY HOUSE OF CARDS

PAGE 34
APRICOT JAM

PAGE 35
BATTLE OF THE BANDS

PAGE 36
SENATOR ELIZABETH WARREN

PAGE 37
1. GREAT FALLS; 2. FALLS BACK;
3. BACK COUNTRY; 4. COUNTRY
CODE; 5. CODE WORD; 6. WORD
PERFECT; 7. PERFECT STORM

ANSWER KEY

PAGES 38-39

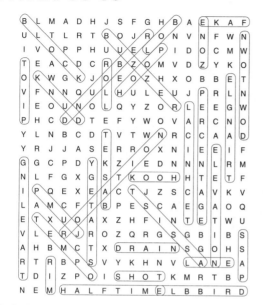

PAGE 40
PAINT BY NUMBERS

PAGE 41

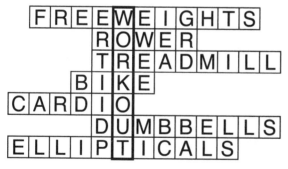

PAGE 42
GOOEY FUDGE

PAGE 43
GREEN PEAS AND BLUE CHEESE

PAGES 44-45

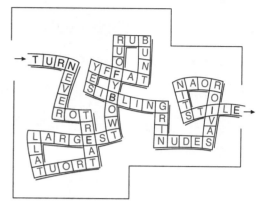

PAGE 46
HARDWOOD FLOORS

PAGE 47
HIGHWAY & SOLAR SYSTEM

PAGE 48

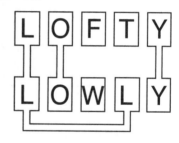

PAGE 49
THE MISSING LETTER IS B.
BRACKET
LAMBKIN
LIMBERS

THE MISSING LETTER IS C.
CONTACT
COUNCIL
CRAZING
CURTAIN

ANSWER KEY

PAGE 50
HOMEMADE MUFFINS

PAGE 51
JOG YOUR MEMORY

PAGE 52
CHUMP CHANGE

PAGE 53

PAGE 54
LATITUDE & LONGITUDE

PAGE 55
MADISON WISCONSIN

PAGE 56
MONARCH BUTTERFLY

PAGE 57
PABLO PICASSO

PAGE 58
1. SILVER; 2. IRON; 3. GOLD;
4. STEEL; 5. BRASS; 6. NICKEL

PAGE 59
A THOUSAND ACRES BY
JANE SMILEY

PAGES 60-61

PAGES 62-63

362

ANSWER KEY

PAGE 64
PERFECTIONIST

PAGE 65
PREHEATING THE OVEN

PAGE 66
QUIRKY QUIZ QUESTIONS

PAGE 67
ROOFTOP GARDEN

PAGE 68
JAMES POLK

L	P	E	M	K	O	A	S	J
A	K	M	J	E	S	O	L	P
O	S	J	L	P	A	M	K	E
K	L	A	O	S	J	E	P	M
P	E	S	A	M	K	L	J	O
J	M	O	P	L	E	K	A	S
E	J	P	K	A	M	S	O	L
S	O	K	E	J	L	P	M	A
M	A	L	S	O	P	J	E	K

PAGE 69
BROADWAY STAR
LIN-MANUEL MIRANDA

PAGES 70-71

PAGES 72-73

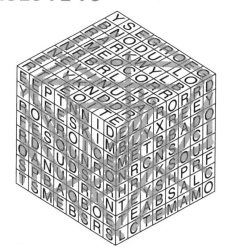

PAGE 74
Q IS FOR QUARRY BY
SUE GRAFTON

363

ANSWER KEY

PAGE 75
A. HYPERACTIVE; B. FOURS;
C. CHILDREN; D. WIFFLEBALL;
E. FOREST; F. MAJORETTE;
G. HONORS; H. ROMEO; I. CARATS

"ANY MOTHER COULD PERFORM
THE JOBS OF SEVERAL AIR TRAFFIC
CONTROLLERS WITH EASE."

PAGES 76-77
NEWLY ENROLLED ROYAL GUARD
SOLDIER AND THREE FRIENDS
BECOME EMBROILED IN POLITICAL
INTRIGUE WHEN THEY CROSS PATHS
WITH MALICIOUS FEMALE SPY
WORKING FOR RUTHLESS CARDINAL.
"THE THREE MUSKETEERS" BY
ALEXANDRE DUMAS

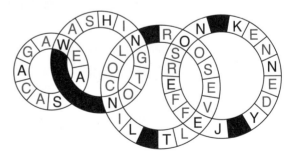

PAGE 78
SETTING UP A LEMONADE STAND

PAGE 79
SOAKING UP THE SUNSHINE

PAGE 80
BLOWING BUBBLES

PAGE 81
BRIDAL REGISTRY

PAGE 82
FRANKENSTEIN BY
MARY SHELLEY

PAGE 83
1. BOOK; 2. STORY; 3. TALE;
4. PLAY; 5. LETTER; 6. NOTE

PAGE 84
SQUIRREL MONKEYS

PAGE 85
STUDY BUDDY

PAGE 86
QUEEN NOOR OF JORDAN

PAGE 87

ANSWER KEY

PAGE 88
SUSHI BAR OF SOAP

PAGE 89
THE AVENGERS

PAGE 90
CAMPING IN THE BACKYARD

PAGE 91
COLLECTING SEASHELLS

PAGE 92
GEORGE WASHINGTON CARVER

PAGE 93
BISCUITS AND GRAVY

PAGE 94
CRACKING JOKES

PAGE 95
DOING THE TANGO

PAGE 96
DOWNTOWN SHOPPING CENTER

PAGE 97
EXTRAORDINARY MAYAN RUINS

PAGE 98

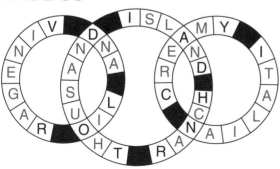

PAGE 99

1	2	3	4	5	6	7	8	9	10	11	12	13
V	N	J	T	A	Y	L	O	R	C	F	I	P

14	15	16	17	18	19	20	21	22	23	24	25	26
M	W	Q	G	D	B	U	S	H	K	X	E	Z

PAGE 100
THE LIBRARY OF CONGRESS

PAGE 101
THRILLING EXPERIENCE

PAGE 102
1. ALMOND PASTE; 2. PASTE JEWELRY; 3. JEWELRY STORE; 4. STOREWIDE; 5. WIDESCREEN; 6. SCREEN NAME; 7. NAME DROPPER

PAGE 103
FRIDAY NIGHT FISH FRY

PAGES 104-105

P	S	S	T		A	M	P	S		G	A	L	A	S
R	I	P	E		R	O	L	L		A	D	O	R	E
O	M	A	N		E	T	U	I		L	D	O	P	A
B	I	R	D	S	N	E	S	T	S	O	U	P		
E	A	T		P	A	T		O	R	P	H	A	N	
S	N	A	R	L			P	Y	R	E		O	N	O
			E	A	R	S	H	O	T		F	L	A	B
		R	A	T	A	T	O	U	I	L	L	E		
S	E	E	M		C	A	T	S	E	Y	E			
A	R	C		T	H	R	O		R	A	M	P	S	
P	S	Y	C	H	E		S	K	I		A	I	M	
	C	H	I	L	I	C	O	N	C	A	R	N	E	
D	O	L	O	R		N	I	N	A		T	O	I	L
O	V	E	R	S		O	T	I	C		T	O	O	L
C	A	D	E	T		N	E	C	K		A	N	N	S

PAGE 106
TOM CRUISE LINER

365

ANSWER KEY

PAGE 107
VIENNA AUSTRIA

PAGE 108
GREEN BEANS ALMONDINE

PAGE 109
1. POTATO; 2. PEPPER; 3. BANANA;
4. BEAN; 5. ONION; 6. RICE

PAGE 110
FIDDLE PLAYER

PAGE 111
FURNITURE DESIGNER

PAGE 112
WORKING UP AN APPETITE

PAGE 113
A SNAIL AND A WHALE

PAGE 114

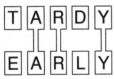

PAGE 115
PEPPERMINT PATTY MELT

PAGE 116
GRADUATION CEREMONY

PAGE 117
HAPPY NEW YEAR!

PAGE 118
1. MINUTE BOOK; 2. BOOK CLUB;
3. CLUB STEAK; 4. STEAK HOUSE;
5. HOUSE PAINT; 6. PAINT ROLLER;
7. ROLLER BEARING

PAGE 119
HERMIT CRAB

PAGE 120

PAGE 121
OATMEAL RAISIN COOKIES

PAGE 122
ANCIENT ARTIFACTS

PAGE 123
BABY GROUNDHOGS

PAGES 124-125

H	A	R	D	■	G	A	P	E	D	■	C	O	C	O

(crossword grid answers)
HARD · GAPED · COCO
ERIE · OLIVE · ARUM
REDSNAPPER · SARI
BASTE · HERA · SNIT
RAGAS · IMAGES
ANGORA · ALIVE
VERY · UPON · TAPAS
EWE · BROWNIE · ESP
STENO · SLAB · METE
NONET · ITALIC
SLOVEN · JADED
PINE · AFAR · CDROM
LAIN · BLUECHEESE
ANOA · LENTO · RALE
TANS · EATEN · SLOT

366

ANSWER KEY

PAGE 126
ROASTED BRUSSELS SPROUTS

PAGE 127
HIPPOPOTAMUS

PAGE 128

1	2	3	4	5	6	7	8	9	10	11	12	13
H	J	O	C	P	A	R	I	S	D	V	F	K

14	15	16	17	18	19	20	21	22	23	24	25	26
Q	Y	N	Z	E	U	T	B	X	M	G	W	L

PAGE 129
TRINIDAD AND TOBAGO

PAGE 130
ISLE OF MAN

PAGE 131

N	L	E	G	I	T	R	V	A
T	R	A	V	E	L	I	N	G
G	V	I	R	A	N	E	T	L
A	N	G	E	V	R	T	L	I
L	E	T	A	N	I	G	R	V
R	I	V	L	T	G	N	A	E
V	G	N	T	L	E	A	I	R
E	T	L	I	R	A	V	G	N
I	A	R	N	G	V	L	E	T

PAGE 132
BIRTHDAY BALLOONS

PAGE 133
BOTTOMLESS & PEACH PIT

PAGE 134
A. SHAWL; B. UNENCUMBERED;
C. SHEAF; D. MYSTERIOUSLY;
E. RATTLESNAKE; F. OATHS;
G. HONEYMOONERS;
H. ADRENALINE
"MAKE YOURSELF AN HONEST
MAN, AND THEN YOU MAY BE
SURE THERE IS ONE LESS RASCAL
IN THE WORLD."

PAGE 135
BOSSYPANTS BY TINA FEY

PAGE 136
BUILDING BRIDGES

PAGE 137
CLINT EASTWOOD

PAGE 138

P	U	B	L	I	S	H	E	R
H	I	L	R	E	B	S	U	P
S	E	R	H	P	U	L	B	I
U	L	S	I	R	H	E	P	B
R	P	H	S	B	E	U	I	L
I	B	E	P	U	L	R	S	H
B	S	I	E	H	R	P	L	U
E	R	P	U	L	I	B	H	S
L	H	U	B	S	P	I	R	E

PAGE 139
1. BROAD SHEET; 2. SHEET MUSIC;
3. MUSIC VIDEO; 4. VIDEO GAME;
5. GAME POINT; 6. POINT BLANK;
7. BLANK SLATE

ANSWER KEY

PAGE 140

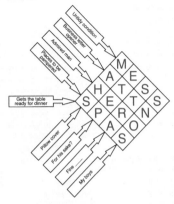

PAGE 141
COURTESY & MATING CALL

PAGE 142
DENVER BRONCOS

PAGE 143
DOWN COMFORTER

PAGE 144
ENGLISH LITERATURE

PAGE 145
FICTIONAL DETECTIVE

PAGE 146
MARGHERITA PIZZA

PAGE 147
1. SHORTER QUARTER; 2. SEAL MEAL; 3. FRUIT SUIT; 4. BOG FOG; 5. WEIRD BEARD; 6. CLAM JAM; 7. EWE HUE; 8. SALT VAULT; 9. WISER MISER; 10. SMART START; 11. SLIM TIM; 12. DENSE FENCE; 13. HEARTY PARTY; 14. GHOST'S BOASTS; 15. TOP COP

PAGE 148
1. PITCH PIPE; 2. PIPE DREAM; 3. DREAM TEAM; 4. TEAM SPIRIT; 5. SPIRIT GUM; 6. GUM ARABIC; 7. ARABIC NUMERAL

PAGE 149
I SPEAK FLUENT FRENCH FRIES

PAGE 150
KICKING OFF MY FLIP-FLOPS

PAGE 151
LOCAL WEATHERMAN

PAGE 152
FRIED PICKLES

PAGE 153
GRACEFUL GAZELLE

PAGE 154
MADE IN THE SHADE

PAGE 155
1. GATES SKATES; 2. BLASS CLASS; 3. MURRAY WORRY; 4. HALEYS DAILIES; 5. CLINTON HINTIN'

PAGE 156
HAPPY CHILDREN

PAGE 157
HARRY POTTER

PAGE 158
HIKING BOOTS

PAGE 159
HUGH JACKMAN

ANSWER KEY

PAGE 160
1. BEST NEST; 2. FEED STEED;
3. HOOD'S WOODS; 4. ACTOR'S
TRACTORS; 5. OPPOSING
PROPOSING

PAGE 161
FAKE IT TIL YOU MAKE IT

PAGES 162-163

PAGE 164

D	A	R	T	S
A	W	A	R	E
F	A	C	E	T
T	Y	K	E	S

PAGE 165
DOVETAILS

PAGE 166
MICROWAVE POPCORN

PAGE 167
NIAGARA FALLS

PAGE 168
GERMAN SHEPHERD DOG

PAGE 169

P	A	S	S	E
A	L	O	N	E
C	O	R	A	L
K	E	E	P	S

ANSWER KEY

PAGES 170-171

PAGE 172
KELLY CLARKSON

PAGE 173
LINCOLN NEBRASKA

PAGES 174-175

PAGES 176-177
The leftover letters spell:
Mediterranean Sea.

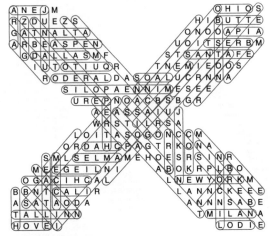

PAGE 178
MEANINGFUL MOMENTS

PAGE 179
MY FAVORITE JACKET

PAGE 180
1. GET IN TOUCH; 2. TOUCHSTONE;
3. STONE-COLD; 4. COLD FEET;
5. FEET FIRST; 6. FIRST LADIES;
7. LADIES NIGHT

PAGE 181
JEEPERS CREEPERS

ANSWER KEY

PAGES 182-183
1. EDITION; 2. ALOUD; 3. ASSENT;
4. OFFAL; 5. BUILD; 6. BRAYED;
7. CASH; 8. CAPITOL; 9. CRUDE;
10. QUEUE; 11. DISCRETE; 12. PHASE;
13. GAMBOL; 14. GOURD; 15. HERD;
16. COLONEL; 17. LAYER; 18. LEAST;
19. MANOR; 20. MUSTERED;
21. PERISH; 22. FLOCKS;
23. PRINCIPLE; 24. STATIONERY;
25. USE AND YEWS; 26. PEEK AND
PIQUE; 27. RAISE AND RAZE

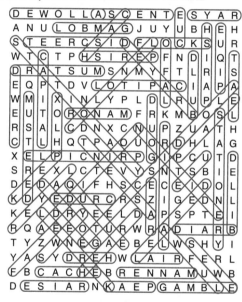

PAGE 184
PACKING MY BATHING SUIT

PAGE 185
PHOENIX AND FLAGSTAFF

PAGE 186
AWESOME POSSUM

PAGE 187
1. ZOO GREW; 2. KNEW LOU;
3. THREW SHOE; 4. VIEW WHO;
5. SLEW GNU

THEME: ALL 10 WORDS IN THE
ANSWERS RHYME WITH EACH
OTHER.

PAGE 188
DRESS FOR SUCCESS

PAGE 189
PADDLING A CANOE

PAGE 190
PRESS CONFERENCE

PAGE 191
RAZZLE-DAZZLE

PAGE 192
SATISFACTION GUARANTEED

PAGE 193
SIBERIAN HUSKY

PAGE 194
PINCH ME I'M DREAMING

PAGE 195
PRICELESS PAINTING

PAGE 196
SPARE PARTS OF SPEECH

PAGE 197
STANDING OVATION

PAGE 198
PRIDE AND PREJUDICE
BY JANE AUSTEN

ANSWER KEY

PAGE 199
ANSWERS MAY VARY.
1. RHYME, THYME, THAME, SHAME, SHAKE, STAKE, STALE, STALL
2. GRIME, CRIME, CLIME, SLIME, SLIDE, SNIDE, SNIPE, SWIPE

PAGE 200
STUNNING COASTLINES

PAGE 201
SWITZERLAND

PAGE 202
1. FAIR SHARE; 2. COOL SCHOOL;
3. BLAST PAST; 4. CLEAN TEEN;
5. PACK SNACK; 6. SQUARE CHAIR;
7. CALF'S LAUGHS; 8. FINER DINER;
9. LOCO COCOA; 10. SLOWER MOWER; 11. STOLE COAL

PAGE 203
1. DAYBREAK; 2. BREAK OPEN;
3. OPEN SESAME; 4. SESAME STREET; 5. STREET LAMP;
6. LAMPLIGHTER; 7. LIGHTER FLUID

PAGE 204
LARGE AND IN CHARGE

PAGE 205

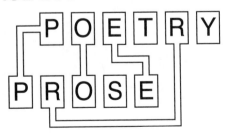

PAGE 206

PAGE 207
PAINT HORSE

PAGES 208-209

PAGE 210
SNOW LEOPARD

ANSWER KEY

PAGE 211
MAN ON A MISSION TAMES NINE LIONS

PAGE 212
REACHING THE FINISH LINE

PAGE 213
SEATTLE WASHINGTON

PAGE 214
THE BIG LEBOWSKI

PAGE 215
THE OREGON COAST

PAGE 216
PITCHER PLANT

PAGE 217

PAGES 218-219

PAGE 220
GANGES RIVER DELTA

PAGE 221
SISTERS AND BROTHERS

PAGES 222-223

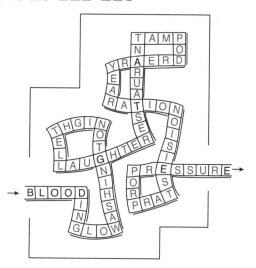

ANSWER KEY

PAGE 224
SPICY CRAB CAKES

PAGE 225
STARFISH AND STINGRAYS

PAGES 226-227

PAGE 228
FLYING SQUIRREL

PAGE 229
SUNSET BOULEVARD

PAGE 230
CHRIS EVANS AS CAPTAIN AMERICA

PAGE 231
ANSWERS MAY VARY.
LIAM, LIAR, LEAR, LEAD, LEND,
LENT, LINT, LIST

PAGE 232
THANK YOUR LUCKY STARS

PAGE 233
THE EIFFEL TOWER

PAGE 234
1. PASSION FRUIT; 2. FRUIT
COCKTAIL; 3. COCKTAIL DRESS;
4. DRESS REHEARSAL;
5. REHEARSAL DINNER; 6. DINNER
THEATER; 7. THEATER CURTAIN

PAGE 235
MERYL STREEP AS JOANNA KRAMER

PAGE 236
THE TIP OF THE ICEBERG

PAGE 237
TO THE BEST OF MY KNOWLEDGE

PAGES 238-239

ANSWER KEY

PAGES 240-241

PAGE 242
PATRICK STEWART AS
JEAN-LUC PICARD

PAGE 243
ANSWERS MAY VARY.
FAYE, RAYE, RAYS, ROYS, ROOS,
ROOD, ROAD, ROAN, JOAN

PAGES 244-245
1. GODFATHER; 2. A BEAUTIFUL MIND;
3. OUT OF AFRICA; 4. RAIN MAN;
5. AMADEUS; 6. MIDNIGHT COWBOY;
7. CASABLANCA; 8. PATTON;
9. MY FAIR LADY; 10. UNFORGIVEN;
11. FORREST GUMP; 12. ROCKY;
13. TITANIC; 14. BRAVEHEART;
15. CHICAGO

PAGE 246
TOSSING AND TURNING

PAGE 247
WINDSURFING LESSONS

PAGE 248
1. BONANZA; 2. BENSON; 3. DALLAS;
4. FRIDAYS; 5. GUNSMOKE;
6. JEFFERSONS; 7. ALICE; 8. QUINCY;
9. TAXI; 10. TOMORROW;

1. CADDYSHACK; 2. CINDERELLA;
3. GREASE; 4. JAWS; 5. ALIEN;
6. MEATBALLS; 7. ROCKY;
8. AIRPLANE; 9. EARTHQUAKE;
10. SUPERMAN

ANSWER KEY

PAGE 249

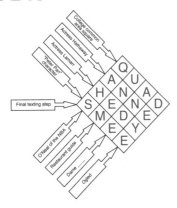

PAGE 250
1. CARROT, ESCAROLE; 2. ERIE, SUPERIOR; 3. SEPTEMBER, NOVEMBER, DECEMBER; 4. SAHARA, KALAHARI; 5. HUNGARY, BULGARIA

PAGE 251
FORT MYERS FLORIDA

PAGES 252-253

PAGE 254
ANSWERS MAY VARY.
OWEN, OWES, OWLS, OILS, MILS, MILE, MULE, MUTE, LUTE, LUKE

PAGE 255
JENNIFER LAWRENCE AS KATNISS EVERDEEN

PAGES 256-257
1. BEN STILLER; 2. NICOLE KIDMAN; 3. JULIA ROBERTS; 4. WILL SMITH; 5. JIM CARREY; 6. BRAD PITT; 7. TOM CRUISE; 8. CAMERON DIAZ; 9. MEL GIBSON; 10. JOHNNY DEPP; 11. MATT DAMON; 12. RUSSELL CROWE; 13. GEORGE CLOONEY; 14. TOM HANKS; 15. SANDRA BULLOCK

ANSWER KEY

PAGES 258-259

PAGES 266-267

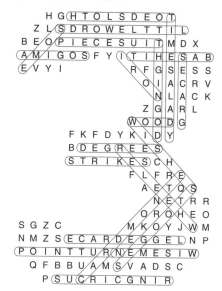

PAGE 260
PAUL NEWMAN AS BUTCH CASSIDY

PAGE 261
ANSWERS MAY VARY.
DATE, DARE, FARE, FIRE, FILE, FILM

PAGE 262
YEARBOOK PHOTOS

PAGE 263
A POD OF DOLPHINS

PAGE 264
THE MISSING LETTER IS Y.
STRATEGY, SYNAPSE, MATERNITY,
WORTHY

THE MISSING LETTER IS U.
RITUAL, NUCLEUS, LUCRATIVE,
ALTRUISM

PAGE 265
GAS GUZZLER

PAGES 268-269

PAGE 270
ADD IT TO MY SHOPPING CART

PAGE 271
ASTOUNDING WATERFALLS

ANSWER KEY

PAGES 272-273

The leftover letters spell: "She inspired her own cocktail. The "Shirley Temple" is a nonalcoholic drink made with ginger ale or lemon-lime soda, grenadine, and orange juice and is garnished with a maraschino cherry and lemon slice."

PAGES 274-275

PAGE 276
JULIANNA MARGULIES AS ALICIA FLORRICK

PAGE 277
BUILDING BLOCKS

PAGE 278

1	2	3	4	5	6	7	8	9	10	11	12	13
H	E	R	A	D	S	V	F	L	J	U	N	O
14	15	16	17	18	19	20	21	22	23	24	25	26
G	I	V	T	B	X	C	K	Y	M	P	W	Q

PAGE 279

VIRTUE
VICE

ANSWER KEY

PAGE 280
SPENDING SPREE

PAGE 281
BEEF & BEAN BURRITO

PAGES 282-283

PAGE 284

PAGE 285
THE MISSING LETTER IS B.
BALANCE
BICYCLE
BLANKET

THE MISSING LETTER IS A.
FUCHSIA
MANDATE
PAPOOSE
SURREAL

PAGE 286
BOLIVIA BRAZIL & ARGENTINA

PAGE 287
BRITISH COLUMBIA

PAGE 288

1	2	3	4	5	6	7	8	9	10	11	12	13
M	X	N	S	J	O	L	I	E	V	A	W	F

14	15	16	17	18	19	20	21	22	23	24	25	26
Y	B	T	P	G	C	R	U	Z	H	D	Q	K

PAGE 289
RABBLE ROUSER

PAGE 290
CHANNING TATUM

PAGE 291
COLLEGE SCHOLARSHIP

PAGE 292
KINGDOM OF BHUTAN

ANSWER KEY

PAGE 293

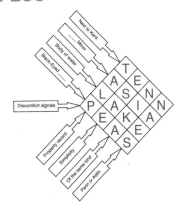

PAGES 294-295

The leftover letters spell: "Italy is one of the great centers of art and fashion."

```
              N M P I
           T A L U A A I Y I E
        S   O N E S S L F Z T
    Y L I C I S T I E O I N Z
    F T O T S A P I T N A M H A
    E F L O R E N C E D T
  G I L L E V A I H C A M
    R O T T E R O T N I T
    C E A     T I L C A D
      E       N S E T S R E
              R O G I E E S
              G O T N N M V
              E F T A A R
              N A O L M A
              O S S E R P S E E
              A R N H A T P
              A C O R Y A
              N P I O N D F A
                L M A     S H
                E C
                C S I
                I U O
                N T N
                E V
```

PAGE 296
CRISPY CRUNCHY CARROTS

PAGE 297
DOLL COLLECTION

PAGE 298

PAGE 299
THE MISSING LETTER IS L.
BARBELL
BRICKLE
CENTRAL

THE MISSING LETTER IS I.
FORENSIC, THIEF, EXAMINE, INVESTIGATE

PAGE 300
DUCKS AND GEESE

PAGE 301
FACE MOISTURIZER

PAGE 302
LOVE LETTER

PAGE 303
AUCKLAND NEW ZEALAND

PAGE 304
FORMULA FOR SUCCESS

PAGE 305
GOING THE EXTRA MILE

ANSWER KEY

PAGE 306
NEW YORK SKYLINE CHILI

PAGE 307
1. PURSE STRINGS; 2. STRINGS ATTACHED; 3. ATTACHED GARAGE; 4. GARAGE SALE; 5. SALE PRICE; 6. PRICE-CUTTING; 7. CUTTING BOARD

PAGE 308
1. LAUGHING GAS; 2. GAS MAIN; 3. MAINLAND; 4. LAND HO; 5. HO-HUM; 6. HUMBUG; 7. BUG-EYED

PAGE 309
ELEMENTARY SCHOOL OF FISH

PAGE 310
GRAND OLE OPRY

PAGE 311
HAPPY WIFE HAPPY LIFE

PAGES 312-313

PAGE 314
SIBERIAN TIGER LILY

PAGE 315
1. KETTLE DRUM; 2. DRUM MAJOR; 3. MAJOR GENERAL; 4. GENERAL STORE; 5. STORE DETECTIVE; 6. DETECTIVE WORK; 7. WORK BENCH

PAGE 316
HIGH SCHOOL NICKNAME

PAGE 317
HOLLYWOOD SCREENWRITER

PAGES 318-319
Leftover letters spell: In all those before-and-after ads, nobody looks worse after.

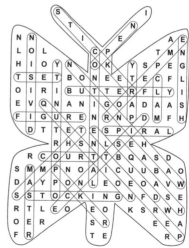

PAGE 320
JAMES BOND MOVIES

PAGE 321
KNITTED SWEATER

ANSWER KEY

PAGES 322-323

PAGE 324
LOOK IT UP IN THE DICTIONARY

PAGE 325
MODERN ART

PAGES 326-327

PAGE 328
ORCHESTRA CONDUCTOR

PAGE 329
PAY IT FORWARD

PAGE 330
1. CURTAIN call; 2. call box;
3. boxcar; 4. car park; 5. park
bench; 6. bench trial; 7. trial RUN

PAGE 331
THE LAST EMPEROR PENGUIN

PAGE 332
PIPING HOT COFFEE

PAGE 333
PURRING KITTENS

PAGE 334
REFRESHING PINEAPPLES

PAGE 335
SERENE AND PRISTINE

PAGES 336-337

PAGE 338
SNOWBOARDING

PAGE 339
SPINACH ARTICHOKE DIP

ANSWER KEY

PAGE 340
HOT AIR BALLOON PAYMENT

PAGE 341
1. LEMON BAR; 2. BAR CODE;
3. CODE RED; 4. RED START;
5. START TALKING; 6. TALKING
HORSE; 7. HORSE SENSE

PAGES 342-343

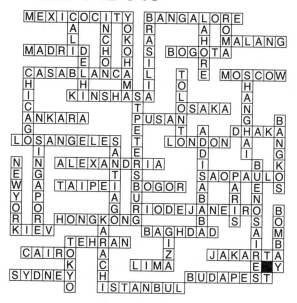

PAGE 344
STOCKHOLM SWEDEN

PAGE 345
SURPRISINGLY SMOOTH SAILING

PAGES 346-347
The leftover letters spell:
"Newfoundland."

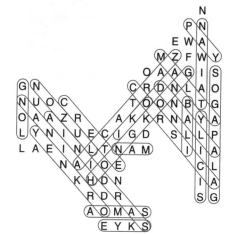

PAGE 348
THE ARCTIC OCEAN

PAGE 349
THE LAS VEGAS STRIP

PAGES 350-351

ANSWER KEY